Collective Imaginings

Collective Imaginings shows us how the work of the seventeenth-century philosopher Benedict de Spinoza is still relevant today. Gatens and Lloyd discuss Spinoza's work from the perspective of a concern with contemporary issues of freedom, responsibility and the understanding of difference.

In re-emphasising the continuities between Spinoza's philosophy and its Stoic sources, this book offers ways of re-thinking contemporary attitudes towards community and difference, freedom and necessity, reason and imagination. We see that what emerges is a concept of responsibility centred less on what we, as individuals, have done than on what we collectively are.

This ground-breaking study will be invaluable reading to students and academics wishing to gain a fresh perspective on Spinoza's thought.

Moira Gatens teaches Philosophy at the University of Sydney. She is the author of *Imaginary Bodies* and *Feminism and Philosophy*. **Genevieve Lloyd** is Professor of Philosophy at the University of New South Wales. She is the author of *The Man of Reason, Being in Time, Part of Nature,* and *Routledge Philosophy Guide to 'Spinoza and the Ethics'.*

Collective Imaginings
Spinoza, past and present

**Moira Gatens and
Genevieve Lloyd**

London and New York

First published 1999 by Routledge
11 New Fetter Lane, London EC4P 4EE

Simultaneously published in the USA and Canada
by Routledge
29 West 35th Street, New York, NY 10001

Routledge is an imprint of the Taylor & Francis Group

Typeset in Times by Routledge
Printed and bound in Great Britain by
St Edmunsbury – St Edmunsbury, Suffolk

British Library Cataloguing in Publication Data
A catalogue record for this book is available from the British Library

Library of Congress Cataloging in Publication Data
Gatens, Moira.
Collective imaginings: Spinoza, past and present / Moira Gatens and
Genevieve Lloyd.
Includes bibliographical references and index.
1. Spinoza. 2. Imagination (Philosophy) 3. Spinoza, Bededictus de,
1632–1677 – Contributions in concept of resposibility. 4.
Responsibility. I. Lloyd, Genevieve. II. Title.
B3999.I3G37 1999   99–13948 CIP
199'.492 – dc21

ISBN 0–415–16570–9 (hbk)
ISBN 0–415–16571–7 (pbk)

Contents

Acknowledgements

This book was completed with the assistance of an Australian Research Council Large Grant. We wish also to express our gratitude for invaluable research assistance provided by Aurelia Armstrong and Justine McGill; for Amir Ahmadi's assistance in the final stages of preparing the manuscript; for helpful comments on earlier versions of chapters provided by Lorraine Code, Douglas Den Uyl, Duncan Ivison, Paul Patton and Amélie Oksenberg Rorty. We benefited from the lively engagement of honours and postgraduate students from the University of Sydney and the University of New South Wales who participated in our Spinoza seminars in 1996 and 1997.

Abbreviations

Abbreviated references to the *Ethics* follow the conventions shown below.

E	*Ethics*
A	Axiom
P	Proposition
D (following a Roman numeral)	Definition
D (following P + an arabic numeral)	the Demonstration of the proposition
C	Corollary
S	Scholium
Exp	Explanation
L	Lemma
Post	Postulate
Pref	Preface
App	Appendix
Def.Aff.	the definition of the affects at the end of Part III

Roman numerals before these abbreviations refer to parts of the *Ethics*.

TP and TTP refer to *Tractatus Politicus* (*Political Treatise*) and *Tractatus Theologico-Politicus* (*Theologico-Political Treatise*), respectively.

Introduction

Why read Spinoza now? Of what value today are the beliefs of a seventeenth-century philosopher who presented his ethical views in geometrical form, and combined his reflections on political practices and institutions with consideration of omens, prophecies and miracles? Underlying this book is the conviction that despite – indeed, because of – its apparent strangeness, the philosophy of Spinoza can be a rich resource for cultural self-understanding in the present. His philosophy is in some respects continuous with dominant assumptions of contemporary Western thought, in others strikingly and illuminatingly discontinuous with them. His philosophy is, in many ways, at odds with what became the philosophical mainstream which has helped form our own thought patterns. This dissonance can serve as the point of departure for articulating alternative ways of conceiving of minds and bodies, of individuals and collectives, and of human power, freedom and responsibility.

Spinoza's philosophy of political life, presented especially in the *Tractatus Theologico-Politicus* and the *Tractatus Politicus*, is wholly grounded in his immanent metaphysics of Nature. And his *Ethics* is just as much a study of the metaphysics of bodies, their causal powers and vulnerability, as it is a treatise on human virtue and happiness. Politics, ethics, epistemology, metaphysics and philosophy of mind are interwoven in his works, and their interconnections raise possibilities of alternative and richer ways of conceptualising contemporary political and social issues. For Spinoza, minds and bodies are united not in causal interactions but in the relations of ideas to their objects. The theory transforms old Aristotelian doctrines of souls as the forms of living bodies, while also pointing the way to new and still undeveloped possibilities.

Spinoza's novel ways of thinking of individual bodies and minds, of their affinities and antagonisms, their harmonies and conflicts, can yield new ways of thinking of individuality and of sociability. In particular, his philosophy allows the modern preoccupation with autonomous individual selfhood to re-connect with ideals of community, without thereby collapsing hard-won individuality into an all-encompassing, pre-existing collective identity. His conjunction of a strong affirmation of freedom with an equally strong repudiation of free will opens up possibilities for re-thinking the relations between individual and collective responsibility. This Spinozistic notion of responsibility moves beyond the common fixation in moral theory on feelings of guilt and the attribution of individual blame. His distinctive treatment of the mind as the 'idea' of the body, rather than as a separate intellectual substance, can allow us to move beyond limitations in the conceptualisation of 'bodily' differences which are the legacy of more influential dualist views. His philosophy points towards new formulations of egalitarian ideals, grounded in the recognition of differences between the powers of socialised bodies, rather than the transcendence of difference, or its assimilation into a universalised sameness.

Spinoza, notoriously, believed that there was only one thing that could truly be said to exist in its own right – one uniquely free-standing Being or 'Substance', known equally as God or as Nature, of which all else is but a modification. This apparently extreme version of philosophical monism is, on the face of it, remote from the assumptions of ordinary consciousness. But in following the movement of thought which Spinoza traced from this idea of Substance to the individuality of minds and bodies, we find, as we shall see, much that resonates with our own contemporary dilemmas in understanding the relations between individual selves and the wider contexts of minds and bodies on which they depend. Spinoza's monism is tempered in two directions: vertically, as it were, in the relations between Substance and its modifications or 'modes', and horizontally – in the relations between individual modes. He insists that this one unique Substance is totally 'expressed' or articulated equally under radically distinct 'attributes' of thought and spatial extension. Neither of these fundamental ways in which the being of Substance unfolds can be reduced to the other; and Substance is totally expressed under each attribute as a multiplicity of irreducibly distinct individual 'modes'.

Spinoza's one unique Substance unfolds as distinct but matching totalities of dynamically interacting modes – an 'order and connection' of modes of thought, which include individual human minds and their ideas, and a corresponding 'order of things' – the totality of finite bodies. Each totality – precisely because each is a complete expression of Substance under one of its attributes – is causally insulated from the other. Nothing that happens in the order of thought depends causally on anything that happens in the order of material things, or vice versa. But the 'order of thought' and the 'order of things' – again precisely because of the status of each as complete expression of Substance – are mapped onto one another in a relation of correspondence. Within the grand scale of these two ordered totalities, the expansion and diminution of the powers of minds match the changing powers of their bodies. Human minds are 'ideas' of human bodies reflecting their persistence and flourishing and their equally complex vulnerability to antagonistic powers. In his appropriation and extension of the concept of *conatus* – the endeavour to persist in being which fascinated also his contemporary Thomas Hobbes – Spinoza develops a rich and resourceful conceptual apparatus, integrating the physics of bodies with the understanding of political relations and institutions which organise and stabilise the differentiated powers of individuals.

Even as Spinoza relies on the language of Aristotelianism, he also lays the groundwork for breaking from these older world views. Other commentators have remarked on Spinoza's tendency to use conventional terminology, including religious terminology, in unconventional and subversive ways.[1] This 'dual language', to use Yovel's phrase (1989a: 29), allows Spinoza to use terms familiar to seventeenth-century philosophy in unfamiliar ways. Becoming acquainted with Spinoza's philosophy involves seeing how his use of Substance (God or Nature) introduces a world view constituted by an infinitely complex network of necessary causal relations. So while there are continuities with older forms of thought, there are also radical breaks. Contrary to Aristotle, Spinoza argues that there are no 'final causes', or no *telos* in Nature. Ends and goals, he argues, are figments of the human imagination, as are notions of free will and an anthropomorphic (loving, angry or judging) God.

In some ways, Spinoza's unorthodox account of Nature brings him closer to our present sensibilities than to those of his own contemporaries. If human life has no natural end, or aim, then the flourishing of human difference, diversity and experimentation become the norm. As we will see, on the Spinozistic world view, normativity itself will take on historically and culturally specific dimensions. The way in which Spinoza theorises the natural order has implications for his understanding of the moral order. Natural right, power and morality figure in his thought in ways which some contemporary readers may find as unsettling as did Spinoza's own contemporaries. In any case, his account of politics, religion and morality have yet to be given the full consideration in contemporary Anglo-American philosophy that it deserves.[2]

This book aims, then, to draw from Spinoza insights which can be put to work in re-conceptualising contemporary understandings of freedom, responsibility, embodied difference and cultural diversity. Central to all these contemporary applications of Spinoza's philosophy is his treatment of imagination, grounded in the direct bodily awareness which is for him constitutive of the mind. In highlighting the positive role of imagination in Spinoza's philosophy, this book departs from some orthodoxies of Spinoza interpretation. His 'rationalism' is often taken as involving a privileging of intellect over supposedly lesser aspects of being human – a transcending of the vagaries of imagination and the turmoil of emotions. It cannot be denied that Spinoza's philosophy brings the operations of imagination under the scrutiny of the critical powers of reason. But Spinozistic imagination, as it is articulated in this book, is double-edged – constructive as well as destructive. Imagination can be a source of distorting illusion, to be remedied by reason, but it can also make good a different kind of deficiency in reason itself. In the interactions between imagination, emotion and intellect, we can see resources that an informed philosophical imagination might bring to the understanding of contemporary issues. Along with his uncompromising rational critique of imagination, superstition and orthodox religion, Spinoza also insists on the positivity of human desire and endeavour. The body, imagination and affect do not, in themselves, represent limits to reason and knowledge. In fact, they are the proper 'objects' of reflection through which we come to develop our powers of reason and increase our knowledge. The crucial distinction in Spinoza's philosophy is not between mind and body, or reason and emotion, but between activity and passivity. Spinoza, rationalist though he was, had a powerful insight not only into the robust resistance imagination can pose to reason but also into the positive role of imagination in even the highest forms of intellectual life.

There are perplexities in our contemporary understanding of our freedom and responsibility, of our individual and collective identities, of our sameness and difference, which arise not at the level of conscious belief but rather from the operations of imagination. Imagery, and the affects that accompany it and that are organised through it, can persist in the form of powerful social fictions even when the explicit beliefs associated with these images and fictions are not consciously endorsed. Reading Spinoza can give us insight into the dominant images and the guiding fictions of contemporary thought as well as into the ways in which our institutions are structured by such affectively invested thought patterns. A Spinozistic approach to imagination and its complex interactions with emotion, desire and intellect can be a powerful tool for opening up possibilities for the social critique of fictions which elude the resources of more conventional criticism.

To read Spinoza is not only to become aware of novel and challenging alternatives to many of the basic thought patterns which we now take for granted. It is also to re-connect with some of the oldest themes and conceptual patterns of Western thought. His works are imbued with ancient philosophies whose concerns and expectations of what was to be gained from intellectual inquiry have largely receded from our own contemporary consciousness. Part I of this book highlights the connections between Spinoza's thought and some ancient Stoic views on the nature of human passions, freedom and responsibility. The very remoteness of these views might seem to make them of little relevance to us here and now. But here again the distinctive mixture of continuity and discontinuity, of familiarity and strangeness which we experience in reading Spinoza raises possibilities for constructively re-activating neglected strands in our philosophical heritage which can revitalise contemporary thought. This book offers a reading of Spinoza which brings the conceptual resources of his philosophy, and of the ancient sources which he creatively appropriated, into living contact with our own present. The contrasts between those ancient sources and our own thought patterns are often stark. But by seeing how Spinoza put his sources to work we can enliven and enrich our own contemporary debates – on freedom and responsibility, on difference and diversity, on the relations between individual and collective dimensions of bodies formed, empowered and restrained by their dynamic interactions and struggles to persist.

As with Spinoza's thought, the contours of contemporary thought are indebted to our philosophical forebears. Contemporary theorists look to the past not only for inspiration but also with a desire to understand how we came to be what we are today. In order to think about the present differently, some understanding of the forces which shaped contemporary thought is required. In Part II, Spinoza's theological and political writings are considered as offering an alternative to contemporary contractualist accounts of human society. This alternative account stresses the powerful role of the imagination in binding together individuals. The resilience of these social fictions lies in their ability to stabilise institutions that, in turn, confer identities on the individuals whom they ostensibly serve. Attaining some understanding of our freedoms and responsibilities in the present depends, at least partly, on understanding these institutional determinations on present identities and differences. How do socialised bodies come to have the powers and capacities that they do? How may informed criticism of institutional arrangements, and the justificatory social fictions which underpin them, contribute to the transformation of present forms of sociability?

Many assumptions underlying our social practices and institutional structures have been strongly influenced by the history of Western philosophy. And many of the anomalies thrown up by the complex interplay of differences in diverse societies arise from clashes between conceptual patterns of which we have little collective reflective understanding. Intelligent readings of formative texts of the Western philosophical tradition have the potential to illuminate patterns of thought and emotional response that structure our implicit expectations, ideals and aspirations. But there are additional gains in reading Spinoza from a contemporary perspective, for he was himself at odds with many of the philosophical assumptions which now inform our own ways of thinking. To read him now is to glimpse hitherto unrealised possibilities of thought.

In an important discussion of the historiography of philosophy, Richard Rorty has distinguished 'past-centred' and 'present-centred' approaches to the history of philosophy (Rorty 1984). In 'present-centred' approaches, philosophers have attempted 'rational reconstructions' of the arguments of past philosophers – an exercise guided by the hope of treating the mighty dead as colleagues with whom they can engage in philosophical debate. On the 'past-centred' approach, in contrast, the aim is to understand past philosophers in their own terms, in relation to their own agenda. The contrast between the two alternatives, Rorty argues, does not really constitute a dilemma: we should do both of these things, but do them separately. There is nothing wrong with self-consciously letting our own philosophical views dictate the terms in which to describe the dead. But there are also reasons to describe them in other terms. We have here, he argues, two different kinds of imaginary conversation; and we can engage in both provided we are clear about what we are doing and why it matters to us. Good history of philosophy needs to try both to reconstruct the conversations past philosophers might have had with their peers, and to bring them into our own contemporary philosophical debates.

Rorty presents his model of conversation as helping to unite concerns which might initially seem at odds: the desire to know ourselves as different from the past, and the desire for continuity. We want to be able to see the history of our thought as 'a long, conversational interchange', and this exercise of the imagination really involves both 'past-centred' and 'present-centred' orientations. We want to understand ourselves as different from our philosophical ancestors. But we want also to assure ourselves that there has been rational progress in the course of recorded history – that we differ from our ancestors on grounds which our ancestors could be led to accept. So we are interested not only in what the Aristotle who walked the streets of Athens could be brought to accept as a correct description of what he had meant or done, but also in what an ideally reasonable and educable Aristotle could be brought to accept as such a description – an ideal Aristotle who can be treated as one of us (Rorty 1984: 51).

The strategies of this book do not fit neatly into either side of Rorty's 'past-centred' and 'present-centred' approaches to the history of philosophy. Although the aim is to bring the philosophy of Spinoza into conversation with the concerns of our present, the agenda for that conversation is not only the 'problems' of contemporary professional philosophy but also the confused cacophony of live discussion of social issues. In addressing the conceptual dimensions of these contemporary debates, the book engages with some of the most fundamental concepts of the Western philosophical tradition. The book does not aim to mine the resources of Spinoza's philosophy for useful tools for re-conceptualising issues which have nothing to do with his own concerns. It aims rather to put Spinoza's own philosophy to work in a context very different from his own. To do that effectively demands respect for the integrity of Spinoza's texts – a willingness to attend to his own voice, in a conversation which takes seriously both his present and our own. This book is then itself an exercise of the philosophical imagination – an endeavour to articulate how an appreciation of Spinoza's philosophy might form the basis of a constructive but critical engagement with contemporary concerns.

This book, then, pursues a third approach which may be described as an exercise in 'critical history', or genealogy. In his book on Foucault, Deleuze succinctly captures the endeavour of the genealogical approach in these terms: '[t]hought thinks its own history (the past), but in order to free itself from what it thinks (the present) and be able finally to "think otherwise" (the future)' (Deleuze 1988b: 119). What Deleuze describes here as a transition from passive thought to a form of thought more aptly described as an ethical activity, resonates with Spinoza's own description of virtue as involving the joyful passage from passivity to activity. This book endeavours to open the past to the present, and through doing so to imagine new ways of conceiving of our freedoms and responsibilities, our compatibilities and our differences, our present and our future.

The challenge of bringing past philosophy to bear on the concerns of a different present is reflected in the structure of this book. Part I offers an account of Spinoza's theory of imagination and of its potential for a contemporary re-conceptualisation of freedom and responsibility. The interpretation of Spinoza offered here emphasises his own re-articulation of ancient philosophical concerns, especially those of the Stoics. In Part II the emphasis shifts to our own use of Spinoza's philosophy in responding to the challenges of the present. Part I gives centrality to the *Ethics*. In Part II, the emphasis shifts to the political writings. But the textual concerns of the two Parts are not sharply separated. Spinoza's political philosophy is grounded to an unusual extent in a broader philosophical treatment of human life – of the natures of minds and bodies, of the relations between individual bodies and wider communities. Central to the reading of Spinoza's philosophy offered in this book is the conviction that these interconnections between politics, ethics, epistemology and metaphysics, yield new insights for addressing contemporary issues. The book's two Parts unfold two temporal orientations: towards Spinoza's own past, in Part I; towards our present and possible future, in Part II. But the two Parts constitute a whole, just as Spinoza's own political philosophy is folded into the metaphysical and ethical concerns addressed in the *Ethics*. The approach to freedom and responsibility sketched in Part I finds fuller expression in the more detailed discussion of contemporary political philosophy in Part II; and the articulation of how truths about the past bear on issues of collective responsibility in the present, discussed in Part II, is grounded in the reading of Spinoza's treatment of imagination presented in Part I. The final version of Part I was written by Genevieve Lloyd and that of Part II by Moira Gatens. But the writing of each Part has issued from a sustained collaboration in researching and teaching Spinoza's philosophy.

In *What is Philosophy?* Deleuze and Guattari wrote: 'If one can still be a Platonist, Cartesian, or Kantian today, it is because one is justified in thinking that their concepts can be reactivated in our problems and inspire those concepts that need to be created' (1994: 28). If this book can be called 'Spinozist', we hope that this is, at least in part, because it engages Spinoza's thought in order to think our present differently. In putting Spinoza's philosophy to work we pay him the tribute of continuing an activity which is in the spirit of his own intellectual *conatus* – an activity of informed philosophical imagination, at the service of social critique.

Part I

Imagination, freedom and responsibility

1   Spinoza's imagination

There is something especially elusive about the history of theories of the imagination. Although the imagination has been central to philosophical deliberation about human knowledge through the centuries, it remains, as Eva Brann puts it in her nonetheless voluminous and illuminating study, a 'missing mystery' in philosophical thought – always the crux, yet rarely the theme of inquiry (Brann 1991: 3). Contemporary theory of imagination reflects this historical elusiveness. Paul Ricoeur has described the contemporary theory of imagination as a shambles – a 'knot of contradictions'. But we should see in its confusion, he suggests, not so much a challenge to produce at last a unified coherent theory, as an expression of a structural complexity in the phenomenon of imagination itself (Ricoeur 1994: 120). Different theories of imagination are then seen as responding to different aspects of a complex human capacity. Rather than attempting to rectify the supposed errors of past theory, it may be more fruitful to explore the different preoccupations reflected in philosophical theory at different times.

This chapter will consider some of the themes from earlier philosophy which come together in Spinoza's version of imagination – the preoccupations to which it responded and the distinctive features of his philosophy which determine it. Later we will see ways in which Spinoza's version of imagination can be appropriated in our contemporary context. Here, as often in the history of philosophy, what we see is not a shift in the answers to stable questions which Spinoza takes over from earlier thinkers. What we find is rather a re-figuration of the capacities of imagination in ways that open up new questions and make possible new relations between philosophical thought and political reality. Spinoza's treatment of the imagination is integrated with his treatment of the nature of mind and its relations with body – with his distinctive account of the individuality of minds and bodies. The distinctive features of this version of imagination cluster around three interconnected themes: the materiality of the imagination; its connections with collectivities and hence with sociability; and its relations with emotion.

Imagination and bodies

Imagination is for Spinoza a form of bodily awareness. That is not novel in the history of philosophy. But bodily awareness here takes on a distinctive form and status as a consequence of Spinoza's treatment of mind and matter as equally attributes of the one Substance – different ways in which the one reality is articulated or 'expressed'. In associating imagination with body, Spinoza does not downgrade it in relation to mind. Mind's immediate confrontation with body is here seen as immediate access to something no less important, no less privileged in relation to ultimate reality than mind itself. The deliverances of imagination are confused; but they connect with modifications of a real attribute of God as Substance.

Imagination thus has for Spinoza a powerful ontological dimension – a direct and strong contact with bodily reality. On the other hand, Spinoza's version of imagination involves an equally strong emphasis on the reality of the mental. The modifications of the mind cannot in this philosophy be seen as an inferior shadowy kind of reality, in comparison with the solidity of the material world. The figments of the imagination are just as real – just as appropriate as objects of systematic investigation – as the modifications of matter. Imagination involves the coming together of mind and body in the most immediate way: mind is the idea of body. Spinoza himself acknowledges the initial strangeness of this way of thinking of the relations between mind and body: 'Here, no doubt, my readers will come to a halt, and think of many things which will give them pause' (EIIP11S). The human mind has for Spinoza the status of an 'idea'; and the object of the idea constituting the human mind is the actually existing human body. It is through imagination that mind has body as its object in the most immediate way. Here minds are constituted as awareness of bodily modifications – modifications through which we are aware of other bodies as well as our own. 'When the human mind regards external bodies through ideas of the affections of its own Body, then we say that it imagines ... and the Mind cannot in any other way ... imagine external bodies as actually existing' (EIIP6D).

Imagination is thus central to the very nature of the mind. But to see the full ethical and political dimensions of Spinoza's version of imagination, we must see imagination also in the context of his treatment of individuality. Each singular finite thing is in this philosophy a particular determination of the power of God as Substance; each mediates the power of Substance and is itself acted upon and changed by the power mediated through other finite things. To be an individual is to be determined to act through the mediation of other finite modes, and to likewise determine others – to act and be acted upon through the totality of finite modes of Substance. All this involves imagination. Spinozistic imagination has a dynamic character which reflects the underlying physics of bodies outlined briefly between Propositions 13 and 14 of Part II of the *Ethics*. Bodies, Spinoza says there, communicate motion to one another; and their synchronisation – the union of bodies – is what constitutes individuality. The simplest bodies are distinguished from one another by motion and rest, speed and slowness. These simple bodies come together as synchronised centres of the communication of motion; and the nested orderings of these composite individuals reach up to the 'whole of nature', conceived as one individual whose parts may vary in infinite ways without any change in the whole (L7S, between EIIP13 and P14). The human body is one such composite individual – a union of parts acting as a centre of communicating and communicated motion. Each individual body exerts a causal force on others, and each is in turn constantly impinged on by others.

The dynamic character of Spinoza's version of individuality is reinforced in later sections of the *Ethics* by his identification of the 'actual essence' of a thing with its *conatus* – the 'striving by which each thing strives to persevere in its being' (EIIIP7). The complexity which results from this account of bodies has its correlate under the attribute of thought – a multiplicity which both enriches the possibilities of human knowing and creates an unavoidable confusion at its very core. 'The human mind is capable of perceiving a great many things, and is the more capable, the more its body can be disposed in a great many ways' (EIIP14). But the source of this enhanced perceptual capacity is the body's dependence on the mediating force of all the other finite bodies which impinge on it. '[T]he human Body requires a great many bodies, by which it is, as it were, continually regenerated' (EIIP19D). The consequences of this dynamic interdependence of bodily modifications are profound.

Spinoza's treatment of the relations between minds and bodies is framed by his treatment of the relations between Substance and attributes, and of the relations between ideas and their objects. Spinoza invites us to consider minds and bodies as it were from two directions. First, on a vertical axis, we can consider minds and bodies as modes of thought and extension respectively, inserted into totalities which completely express the being of God or Substance. Second, there is a horizontal axis – the relations between minds and bodies which hold across the difference between the two attributes. Minds and bodies are united not in causal relations but through the relations of ideas to their objects. Causal relations for Spinoza hold only between modes under some one attribute; there is no possibility of causal relations across the difference between attributes.

The body, of which mind is the 'idea', is not insulated from the rest of nature; it is not a self-contained whole within the totality of the material world. In being aware of its body, the mind is aware not just of one material thing but of other bodies impinging on that body. It is aware, that is, of its own body together with other bodies and of other bodies together with its own. The mind, as idea of the body, incorporates ideas of other bodies; and those ideas can involve awareness of transitions to greater and less states of activity under the influence of congenial and rival forces. This experience of other bodies together with our own is the basis of imagination. But it is also the basis of Spinoza's account of the emotions or 'affects'. Where those bodies are like our own – human bodies which undergo similar modifications – this experience of other bodies can intensify our awareness of our own desires, joys and pains. Already, Spinoza's treatment of minds and bodies evokes a basic sociability which is inseparable from the understanding of human individuality. To see what is distinctive about it it is helpful to have some understanding of how Spinoza draws on and transforms themes which were familiar from older treatments of imagination.

Spinoza's historical sources

Spinoza's treatment of minds and bodies echoes, both in its content and in its rationale, some of the concerns of ancient philosophy. Like Aristotle, Spinoza emphasises the cognitive role of imagination. But his version of imagination echoes also Epicurean and Stoic philosophy, which had a broader agenda than Aristotle's preoccupation with affirming against the Platonists the understanding of individual material things as genuine objects of knowledge. Spinoza's physics of bodies echoes themes from ancient Epicurean atomism; and his philosophy resonates also with the rich and strange Epicurean treatment of images which that atomism grounded. Spinoza's talk of the 'simplest bodies' evokes older Epicurean talk of *primordia* – the imperceptible elements out of which perceptible objects are composed. For the Epicureans, mind, soul and spirit, no less than bodies, were composed of such *primordia*. The Roman poet Lucretius, in his Epicurean poetic work *The Nature of Things*, describes them as wandering through the void, carried either by their own weight, 'like raindrops through the profound void' or by a chance blow from other atoms, arising from unpredictable 'swervings' which disrupt the steady downward motion of the atoms falling under their own weight.[1]

The Epicurean world arises from these imperceptible whirlings and swervings of atoms. In Lucretius's illustrations, just as the movement of sheep or of an army on a distant hill is blurred in our perception, so that we perceive only whiteness or brightness at rest on a plain, so too the mind cannot discern the motion of the *primordia* involved in its perception of objects close by. On the Epicurean theory, the perceiving mind is itself composed of such *primordia* – in this case especially small particles lying deep within us. Mind and spirit are made up of 'very minute seeds' which cling together during life with the coarser particles which make up the body. The spirit seeds give rise to sensation, which thus involves conjoint motions of body and spirit particles – both equally material – though of different size.[2] At death, these smaller seeds separate out from the coarser, bodily particles.

The unexplained conjoint motion of particles provides the frame for the Epicurean account of imagination. Lucretius talks of images as *simulacra* – thin films of atoms drawn from the outermost surfaces of things to 'flit about hither and thither through the air'. These fixed outlines have a shape or look similar to the things which have thrown them off. These images can 'assail' the mind, terrifying it – especially when it is helpless in sleep – with 'wonderful shapes and images of the dead'.[3] They may be 'loosely diffused abroad', as wood throws off smoke and fire heat, or they may be more 'close-knit and condensed', like the neat coat dropped by the cicada in summer, the caul shed by the new-born calf, or the skin shed by the slippery serpent.[4]

There are important differences between Spinoza's materialist version of imagination and the ancient Epicurean version. In assimilating images to material *simulacra*, the Epicureans make perception and imagination passive conditions, in which the mind is invaded or assailed. Spinoza's version of the motion of simple bodies emphasises in contrast the dynamic momentum of the simple bodies, whose very definition is in terms of motion and rest. These bodies, rather than assailing the mind, are its proper objects. Minds, rather than being composed of minute bodies, are 'ideas' of bodies – corresponding modes of substance under the attribute of thought. The materiality of sensation and imagination comes not from an intermingling of differently sized particles, but from the relations between ideas and the bodies which are their object.

There are undoubtedly problems in the Epicurean treatment of imagination, if we look at it as an exercise in epistemological theory. It remains unexplained how sensation arises from the 'conjoint motion' of the *primordia* that make up the mind, with the alien but intermingling *primordia* that assail it. Brann comments dismissively that the theory 'simply bypasses in its violent purity whatever is perplexing in the experience of having images' (Brann 1991: 48). But the agenda of the Epicurean concern with imagination is wider than the clarification of the cognitive operations of the mind. The Epicureans were concerned to allay the superstitious dread that the soul might continue to exist in a tormented afterlife – a fear that could intrude on the enjoyment of life before death. They sought therefore to explain the haunting appearances of the dead to the living in ways that would allay the fear that they were visitations from the realm of the dead. Spinoza's treatment of imagination, as we shall see, is similarly integrated with a concern with understanding and responding to the emotional dimensions of human life. But, within the frame of his view of the mind as idea of the body, these connections between imagination and emotion resonate with some of the themes of ancient Stoicism no less than with Epicurean materialism.

Stoics and Epicureans alike brought together cognitive theory with more practical and ethical concerns. Whereas the Epicureans stress the ontological givenness – the materiality – of imagination, the Stoic concern is rather to emphasise the reality of the mental in order to allow a detachment from what lies beyond the mind's control. The Stoics, too, believed in material elements. But where the Epicurean model conjures up a mind assailed by external whirling particles, the Stoic treatment of imagination stresses the mind's own activity. Spinoza's philosophy allows for both passivity of mind under the onslaught of 'external' causes and for its activity, exerted in the understanding of those causes. The transitions between these states of passivity and activity are central, as we will see, to Spinoza's treatment of freedom. There we see him integrate ethical and cognitive dimensions of mental activity and passivity – an integration which centres on the role of imagination. The mind's capacity to gain freedom from the vicissitudes of passion is bound up with its capacity to represent to itself, and hence to gain understanding of, what is not actually presented to it in immediate bodily modification – of what is absent or no longer existent.

In the background to Spinoza's treatment of the cognitive capacities of the imagination is the Aristotelian concept of *phantasma* – the mental representations through which the mind exercises its capacity to know individual material things. In the thought of the Stoics the operations of the imagination were articulated in terms of a set of related notions, centred on a notion of 'impression' – *phantasia* – derived from ideals of light and illumination. The Stoic distinctions serve to emphasise the dual role of imagination. On the one hand, it gives the mind access to material particulars presented to it for knowledge; on the other, it allows the mind to think of what is not presented to it. The crucial distinctions here are attributed to Chrysippus. The early Greek doxogropher, Aetius, speaks of him as drawing a fourfold distinction. The 'impression' (*phantaston*) is an 'affection' occurring in the soul, which 'reveals itself and its cause', just as light reveals both itself and whatever is included in its range. The cause of the impression is the 'impressor' (*phantasticon*) which 'activates' the soul, as something white or cold activates perception. Then there is 'imagination' (*phantastikon*), which is described as an 'empty attraction' – an 'affection in the soul which arises from no impressor, as when someone shadow-boxes or strike his hands against thin air'; and the 'figment' (*phantasma*) – 'that to which we are attracted in the empty attraction of imagination', which occurs in people who are 'melancholic and mad' (Long and Sedley 1987: 237).

What is important for our purposes here is the notion of 'empty attractions' – the 'impressions' for which there are no 'impressors', the 'shadow boxing' of the mind. To see the implications of this metaphor we have to resist reading back into Stoic thought more familiar modern ideas of causal interaction between inner mental life and external bodily world. The Stoics did think of the relations between 'impressors' and 'impressions' as a causal one. But the causal relation is not here aligned with the distinction between bodies and minds as we now understand it. 'Bodily' things are whatever is capable of standing in a causal relation to mind; but this is a much broader class of things than those we would now think of as bodies. 'Bodily' things for the Stoics included things which are not in our modern understanding physical – virtue and the gods, for example. Nor is the Stoic notion of 'impression' aligned with what is the effect of a cause; there is a category of 'incorporeals' in relation to which the soul can be 'impressed' in a relation that is not causal. What the Stoics called the 'sayables' are a sub-class of 'impressors' which are non-causally related to 'impressions': the mind is 'impressed' in relation to them, but not *by* them, as in a causal relation.[5]

The mind's imaginative power to think of what is not there – to be 'impressed' without being activated by an 'impressor' is for the Stoics manifested both as madness and as reason – as the vulnerability to illusion and as the capacity to understand universal concepts. Not all 'figments' are illusory. Universal concepts such as 'man', for example, are called 'figments' because they have no corresponding 'impressor': there is no generic 'man' which activates the mind when it grasps a universal concept. Spinoza's philosophy emphasises the nexus between these two aspects of the imagination; and his treatment of this dual role of the imagination resonates with themes of activity and passivity from Epicurean and Stoic sources. In his version of the mind's capacity to think what is not there the awareness of bodily complexity is fundamental. In sensation, Spinoza stresses, our minds perceive the nature of a great many bodies together with the nature of our own. In other words, our perceptions are confused, and the confusion carries over into imagination and memory. The human body is of a higher degree of complexity than other bodies, incorporating a greater number of subordinate unities; and this greater complexity makes it capable of acting and being acted upon in many ways at once.

Spinoza's treatment of sensation, memory and imagination is grounded in this bodily complexity. Our bodies retain traces of the changes brought about in them by the impinging of other bodies. So the mind will again regard external bodies as present even when they no longer exist (EIIP17D and C). These ideas of affections of the body which present external bodies as present to us are Spinoza's version of images; and the mind's regarding bodies in this way is his version of imagining. Paul's mind will continue to regard Peter as present to it, even after Peter's death, when the idea of Peter which constitutes Peter's mind no longer exists. There is no question here of the idea of Peter flitting around the world independently of Peter, to find its way into the mind of Paul. Spinoza's images are not Epicurean *simulacra*. Yet there is in Spinoza's version of imagination a materiality which retains something of the Epicurean account. There is also, however, an equally strong emphasis on the power of the mind, which echoes the Stoic theories and leads into a new version of the Stoic ideal of detachment from what lies outside the mind's own activity. Let us now see how these ancient concerns with gaining freedom through over-coming superstition and illusion are re-enacted and transformed in Spinoza's treatment of imagination.

The letter to Balling: imagination and omens

On 20 July 1664, Spinoza wrote a response to a letter from his friend Pieter Balling about the death of his son.[6] Spinoza's letter refers to his friend's capacity to withstand 'the blows of fortune, or rather opinion'. The point of the disjunction becomes clearer as the letter proceeds: what has assailed Balling is not only grief at mortality; under the sway of grief, he has found himself drawn to a belief – distressing in its apparent irrationality – in omens.

In the letter to which Spinoza's is a response, Balling reported that when his child was still well, he heard sighs like those which the child uttered shortly before his death – sounds which he no longer heard when he got up to investigate. Looking back he ponders whether the sighs were an omen – a portent, not understood, of what lay in the unknown future. Spinoza's response begins with a reassurance which may well, from our modern perspective, seem unnecessary. 'I should think', he says, 'that this was not a true sigh, but only your imagination.' Spinoza then proceeds to offer an analysis of the operations of imagination which produce such experiences. The point is not just to deflect his friend's preoccupations into a more positive intellectual inquiry which may distract him from his grief. Spinoza is attempting to reassure his grieving friend about an experience which has shaken his confidence in the rationality of the world and of his own mental processes.

The content of the analysis which unfolds is not just incidentally related to the fact that it occurs in a sympathy letter to a grieving friend. Spinoza engages seriously with Balling's experience, drawing out the interrelated operations of imagination and emotion which have produced it – offering a rational explanation, at the core of which is the intensity of the father's love which now takes the form of grief. Spinoza reassures his friend that the 'omen' arose from his imagination. But having relocated the phenomenon from the world of real events to the mental realm, Spinoza does not dismiss its importance – or indeed its status as 'omen'. Rather, he offers a detailed explanation, laying down rational principles for the conditions under which such an event can be treated as a confused apprehension of the future. To locate the omen as belonging to the imagination – rather than as something physical – is, it emerges, not to deny its reality. On the contrary, it allows that reality to be properly investigated. By understanding the operations of his imagination, Balling will be released from the false opinion about fortune which has assailed him.

The fascinating thing for a modern reader here is that, having been relocated into the imagination, the reality of omens does not simply disappear. The omen becomes a proper object for understanding – not just as an insignificant illusory appearance, but as indeed an 'omen'; that is, as a genuine intimation of the future which the rational mind need not spurn. What Spinoza wants to make clear is that the operation of the omen is misunderstood if it is interpreted in terms of physical reality. The letter confronts us with an initially disconcerting way of thinking of the relations between different kinds of connection between past, present and future. To regard omens as belonging with the operations of causal processes in the physical world threatens the rational understanding of that world. In the grip of such a superstitious belief the mind is vulnerable to what it sees as 'blows of fortune' – blows which would be better understood, according to Spinoza, as blows of distorting 'opinion'. By removing that misunderstanding of omens, relocating them into the realm of imagination, we attain freedom from the onslaught of false opinions. But omens – with their reference to the future – are not shed in Spinoza's analysis of the kind of experience his friend has been through. Rather, they are reconstructed in a way that reveals them to be no threat to reason.

Spinoza goes on to bring the point out by comparing his friend's experience with one of his own, which he regards as, unlike Balling's, not an omen. Waking once from a deep dream, he reports, he found the dream images remained before his eyes as vividly as if the thing had been true – especially the image of 'a certain black, scabby Brazilian'. As with Balling's auditory images, the appearance of the Brazilian depends on the mind's not being in a state of attention. Just as the sighs heard by his friend disappear when he gets up to investigate, Spinoza's visual image disappears when he fixes his attention on a book, returning with the same vividness when his attention strays, until it gradually vanishes from his visual field.

Spinoza's explanation of why the one experience, and not the other, is an omen is revealing. The effects of the imagination, he says, arise from the constitution either of the body or of the mind. Fevers can cause madness; thickness of the blood can make us imagine quarrels, troubles and killings. But the imagination can also be determined by 'the constitution of the soul alone'. The imagination 'follows the traces of the intellect in everything', linking its images and words together in order, as the intellect links its demonstrations. We can hardly understand anything, Spinoza concludes, of which the imagination does not form some image from a trace. Imagination and intellect are here presented as involving two separate orders of thought. But whereas the intellect links together 'demonstrations', what the imagination links

together is 'images and words'. Omens depend on this distinctive associative power of imagination. The effects of the imagination which
proceed from corporeal causes can not, he says, be omens of the
future; for their causes do not involve any future things. However,
images which have their origin in the constitution of the mind can be
omens, because the mind can 'confusedly be aware, beforehand, of
something which is future'. Omens, in other words, are not physical
events causally connected with other, later events. Spinoza directs his
correspondent's attention away from physical events to the relations
between images. The associations between images are important in
understanding omens. Spinoza retains also an element of causality in
his analysis of omens; but it is relocated to the mind's relations with
body, rather than the relations between physical events. The father,
because of his close awareness, grounded in love, of his son's body can
discern in it intimations of what is to come that are not yet perceptible
as present illness.

The capacity to apprehend – however confusedly – the future,
may well strike modern readers as a strange power to attribute to
the imagination. This is partly because we tend to think of the
future as independent of what goes on in human minds. For
Spinoza, as we shall see later, the very idea of the future is bound
up with the operations of imagination. The sense of strangeness is
accentuated by the fact that he is writing against the background –
largely alien to our own ways of thought – of ancient Stoic notions
of sympathy and antipathy operating between different parts of the
world. Commenting, in the *Ethics*, on the differences between his own
way of thinking of these notions and the ancient sources, he says that
the authors who first introduced the words 'sympathy' and 'antipathy'
intended to signify by them occult qualities of things; but that he
believes nevertheless, that 'we may be permitted to understand by them
also qualities that are known or manifest' (EIIIP15S). We can retain
the insight while repudiating the occult notions through which the
ancient philosophers articulated it. His own concern, he says, is with
how it is that we can be affected by things just because they are like
others that have affected us – with 'how it can happen that we love or
hate some things without any cause known to us, but only (as they say)
from Sympathy or Antipathy' (EIIIP15C and D).

In the letter to Balling, Spinoza's account of omens in terms of the
operations of the imagination arising from mind rather than body
emphasises two things that will later, in the *Ethics*, be explored in relation to sympathy and antipathy: the mind's confused awareness of the
future involves emotion and also community. In the case of Balling's

experience, the father 'so loves his son that he and his beloved son are, as it were, one and the same'. Omens are in effect premonitions, confused intimations of the future, which arise from states of strong emotion in relation to others with whom we form a wider whole. To apprehend the future there must be in thought, he continues in the letter, an idea of the son's essence. Because the father by the union he has with his son is a part of the son, the father's soul must necessarily 'participate in the son's ideal essence, its affections, and consequences'. Because he thus 'participates ideally' in his son's essence the father can sometimes imagine what follows from the son's essence as vividly as if he is in its presence. The conditions which Spinoza puts on this capacity of the imagination are that the future incident will be 'remarkable'; that it can be easily imaginable; that it be not very remote in time; and – echoing his previous distinction between imagination as it arises from body and from mind – that the father's body be 'well constituted' and free of 'all cares and troubles that disturb the senses externally'.

Spinoza concludes by linking the phenomenon of omens to something which may appear from our modern perspective more commonplace – the association of ideas, the connections the mind forms between images and affects. In understanding omens, he says, it helps to think of the things which 'for the most part arouse ideas like these'. 'For example, if, while we are speaking with this or that man, we hear sighs, it will generally happen that when we think again of that same man, the sighs we heard when we spoke with him will come into our memory.' For Spinoza it is the same operations of imagination that explain both omens and the formation of habitual associations of ideas which underlie the possibility of human language. They belong, it is true, with operations of mind which do not follow the order of reason. But these operations are understandable through reason. Balling's experience of the omen, moreover, is an expression of something which is of itself a source of joy: the mind's capacity to participate in the essence of those it loves – the capacity to form strong emotional bonds in which individuals come to form part of wider wholes. Balling's omen is not, as the superstitious would have us believe, an eruption into the rational order of something inexplicable. It should be seen not as an additional threat to the rational mind afflicted by grief but as an unthreatening reflection of the father's intense love for his son. Nor does it indicate any malfunctioning of the father's bodily constitution. It arises on the contrary from an 'ideal participation' in his son's essence, which presupposes that the father's own physical constitution is sound.

Later, in the yet to be written concluding sections of the *Ethics*,

Spinoza will develop similar thoughts into an account of the mind's eternity – directed to achieving a reconciliation to death which does not depend on the superstitious belief in an afterlife. In the spirit of the Epicureans, Spinoza has recast a frightening phenomenon, allaying its terrors by providing a rational explanation. The strategy echoes also something of the spirit of the Stoic affirmation of the mental, with its reassuring intimations of the mind's power to resist what appear to be inexorable onslaughts of fortune simply through better understanding mind itself, shedding the false beliefs that intensify its pains. But there are distinctive features of Spinoza's version of the allaying of fear through understanding, which spring from his playing off against one another the equal realities of mind and body as attributes of the one substance. Let us now see how he develops the interconnections of imagination, emotion and sociability in the *Ethics* and the *Theologico-Political Treatise*.

Imagination, emotion and sociability in the *Ethics* and the *Tractatus Theologico-Politicus*

Spinoza's version of imagination has an unavoidably social dimension, which links the metaphysical concerns of the *Ethics* with the more direct social orientation of the political writings. The relations between individuals and wider collectivities are fundamental to the *Ethics* no less than to the political writings; and the treatment of the imagination is fundamental to how Spinoza conceptualises those relations.

For him, as we have seen, imagination involves awareness of other bodies at the same time as our own. Our bodies retain traces of the changes brought about in them by the impinging of other bodies. On this co-presence of things to mind, arising from the structural complexity of the human body, rests the world of ordinary consciousness delivered to us by imagination and memory. A representation can thus be non-actual, in that it has no present cause – no 'impressor' as the Stoics would have said – yet actual, in that it involves the absent or now non-existent thing being present to it. Summing up this bodily grounding of imagination Michèle Bertrand says that for Spinoza 'the body forgets nothing' (Bertrand 1983: 66).

Spinoza defines memory as 'a connection that is in the mind according to the order and connection of the affections of the human Body'. This is a different order from that of clear and distinct ideas of reason, which are organised according to a logical sequence and a relation of perfect correspondence between ideas and their corresponding objects – modes of the same substance under the different attribute of extension. The order of imagination is not the order of reason. But reason can come to an understanding of the associations which operate between images, of the ways in which they are affected by emotion, and of the ways in which those interactions of imagination and emotion are themselves affected by the collectivities into which human beings are drawn through interaction with bodies similar to their own. Our awareness of other human bodies – of the modification of other bodies which are like our own – takes on a special importance here for the individual mind's self-awareness and self-preservation. In the later parts of the *Ethics* Spinoza addresses the patterns of association in which the images and affects of bodies reinforce and obstruct the striving by which all things endeavour to persist in being. The affects of 'hate, anger and the like, considered in themselves', he says, follow with the same 'necessity and force of nature' as anything else we may study. In the preface to Part III, he presents himself as considering 'human actions and appetites' just as if it were a question of 'lines, planes and bodies' (EIIIPref).

Some commentators have interpreted Spinoza's rationalism as in effect denying the reality of the non-rational – as dismissing as unreal whatever cannot be accommodated to the rational order of geometry. Roger Scruton, for example, takes Spinoza as committed to purging the world of all reference to the 'subjective viewpoint from which it is surveyed', rising above the 'illusory perspective' of temporality to the 'absolute viewpoint which is God's' (Scruton 1986: 72–3). On that interpretation, all that is real in 'human actions and appetites' is what can be grasped through rational principles: the non-rational residue is dismissed as unreal. But the inquiry that follows Spinoza's remarks in the preface – although its format does follow a geometrical model, set out with definitions, axioms, demonstrations and corollaries – is in its content a shrewd analysis of the workings of passions: of their inexorable twists and turns, their reinforcements under the force of other passions, their inevitable conflicts and vacillations. Spinoza's point is that human actions and appetites are as real as the bodies whose dynamic structural powers underlie them. To understand the interactions of affect and imagination is not to make human actions and appetites disappear into lines and solids. It is to exert rational understanding on aspects of human life which have hitherto been treated as unworthy of serious investigation. As Antonio Negri sums up this aspect of Spinoza's philosophy, reason now 'traverses the imagination, liberating the truth it contains' (Negri 1991: 106). Spinoza's material for analysis becomes 'the very world of delirium or the most fantastic or crazy dimension of opinion' (Negri 1991: 36). The interactions of passions and imagination here come into view as fitting objects for rational investigation.

The possibility of this rational investigation of what is of itself non-rational rests on the underlying commonalities of human bodies. Spinoza studies the associations which are formed on the basis of those commonalities – the reinforcement of their shared strivings through the forming of larger associations between bodies. If all associations of ideas were circumscribed by the vagaries of individual bodies in their paths through the world, there would be no possibility of finding such ordered patterns. The affections of individual bodies, Spinoza says, lay down widely divergent associational paths. From traces of a horse seen in the sand, the soldier passes to thought of horsemen and war, the farmer to ploughs and fields (EIIP18S). But although these patterns are individual and idiosyncratic – multiple, in contrast to the unitary order of reason – the variations are not a product of the affections of individual bodies in isolation from others. Farming and military activity give rise to different associational paths which reflect different practices.

Spinoza returns to the variations in the patterns of association in the imagination in the early sections of the *Tractatus Theologico-Politicus*. Here, echoing the connections between omens and imagination discussed in the letter to Balling, Spinoza frames his treatment of imagination with a discussion of prophecy. The power of prophecy, he argues, implies not a 'peculiarly perfect mind', but a 'peculiarly vivid imagination' (TTP: 19). The deliverances of prophecy vary according to the disposition, and the preoccupations of the individual prophet:

> If a prophet was cheerful, victories, peace, and events which make men glad, were revealed to him; in that he was naturally more likely to imagine such things. If, on the contrary, he was melancholic, wars and massacres, and calamities were revealed; and so, according as a prophet was merciful, gentle, quick to anger, or severe, he was more fitted for one kind of revelation or another. It varied according to the temper of imagination in this way: if a prophet was cultivated he perceived the mind of God in a cultivated way, if he was confused he perceived it confusedly. And so with revelations perceived through visions, if a prophet was a countryman he saw visions of oxen, cows and the like; if he was a soldier, he saw generals and armies; if a courtier, a royal throne, and so on.
>
> (TTP: 30)

The patterns of association arising from occupational habits and dispositions feed into the differing 'temper of imagination', the distinctive amalgams of imagination and affect. There can be conflict then between the chains of association in different minds; and also within the same mind at different times. These conflicts are expressed as fluctuations of imagination and hence, on Spinoza's definition, fluctuations in the affects of hope and fear, which are the core of political life. The mind of its nature strives to increase its powers and to distance itself from those affects which will diminish its powers. There emerges here an associative logic which could be just as appropriately described as a logic of emotion, and especially of desire, as it can be described as a logic of imagination.[7] The conjoint operations of imagination and emotion are not to be dismissed as mere distortions of reason. The interactions of imagination with the central emotions – desire, joy and sadness – yield systematic variations in intensity of attachment and aversion. These fluctuations are different from the ordered relations between clear and distinct ideas of reason; but they have nonetheless an order of their own which lends itself to rational investigation.

The rational understanding of this affective logic of the non-rational becomes the core of Spinoza's analysis of the forms of political life – analyses which centre on understanding the organisation of the passions rather than on the deliberations of a supposedly rational will. Spinoza sees the passions as operating in conjunction with images, around which they are organised; and he sees these organised patterns of affect and image as changeable through challenging the appropriateness of the images at their core. This gives his analysis of the operations of passions and imagination a practical and ethical orientation which echoes, again, his ancient philosophical sources.[8]

The unities of imagination and affect which are the core of Spinoza's understanding of sociability and politics are grounded in the crucial concept of *conatus* – the endeavour or struggle to persist in being – which informs also his treatment of individuality. We saw before that imagination, like the emotions, is driven by *conatus*. It is this shared dependence on *conatus* that unifies affects and imagination. Joy, sadness and desire are the core of Spinoza's account of the passions, integrated into the very definition of what it is to be a passion at all. Spinoza's general definition of the passions of the mind is that they are confused ideas 'by which the mind affirms of its Body, or of some part of it, a greater or lesser force of existing than before, which, when it is given, determines the Mind to think of this rather than that' (EIIIGen.Def.Aff.). The definition, he goes on to point out, incorporates his understanding of the natures of joy ('a man's passage from a lesser to a greater perfection' (EIIIDef.Aff.II)), sadness ('a man's passage from a greater to a lesser perfection' (EIIIDef.Aff.III)), and desire ('the determination of a man's essence from an affection of it to do something' (EIIIDef.Aff.1)).

Desire thus understood is for Spinoza man's very essence insofar as it is conceived to be determined, from any given affection of it, to do something. Spinoza's concept of desire is closely connected with the concept of *conatus*, which he sees as the very essence of finite individuals. To be an individual is, as we saw earlier, to be determined to act through the mediation of other finite modes, and likewise to determine those others. Since imagination is by definition the awareness of our own bodies together with others, this interaction between bodies essentially involves imagination. But this bodily awareness which is the very nature of imagination is also closely bound up with *conatus*. Bodies and minds, as finite individuals, struggle, of their very nature, to persist in being. Our bodies are not just passively moved by external forces. They have their own momentum – their own characteristic force for existing. But this is not something that individuals exert of their own power alone. For an individual to preserve itself in existence, as we have seen, is precisely for it to act and be acted upon in a multiplicity of ways. The more complex the individual body, the more ways in which it can be affected and affect other things. The power to imagine is thus integral to the continued existence and thriving of the individual. To define imagination in terms of bodily awareness, within the context of Spinoza's philosophy, is to move imagination to the very centre of the story of human well-being and flourishing.

The operations of imagination are caught up in the dynamics of *conatus* – in the momentum and impetus of the mind in its struggle to enact its nature as a finite individual. And the mind's joys and sorrows, its loves and hates, are here inseparable from the effort to imagine. 'The mind strives to imagine only those things which posit its power of acting' (EIIIP54).

> Insofar as it can, the Mind strives to imagine those things that increase or aid the Body's power of acting ... i.e. ... those it loves. But the imagination is aided by what posits the existence of a thing, and on the other hand, is restrained by what excludes the existence of a thing. ... Therefore, the images of things that posit the existence of a thing loved aid the Mind's striving to imagine the thing loved, i.e. ... affect the Mind with Joy. On the other hand, those which exclude the existence of a thing loved, restrain

the same striving of the Mind, i.e., ... affect the mind with Sadness. Therefore, he who imagines that what he loves is destroyed will be saddened.

(EIIIP19)

Where we imagine another to be like us, sadness, accompanied by the idea of an evil which has happened to them, takes on a social dimension as pity. In Parts III and IV of the *Ethics*, Spinoza offers a systematic elaboration of the interactions between imagination and emotion, and of the ways those interactions are intensified by relations of sympathy and antipathy between people. To understand the operation of the passions in individual life is at the same time to understand the relations of collaboration and antagonism which bind human beings together in society.

Imagination and time: hope, fear and contingency

Emotion and imagining work together; our imaginings are intensified by our loves and hates, and implicated in our fears and hopes. It is in Spinoza's treatment of the operations of hope and fear that we see most clearly the integration of his political philosophy with his metaphysics of human bodies. This was the basis of Spinoza's analysis of the experience of omens in the Balling letter. In the *Ethics* and the *Tractatus Theologico-Politicus*, he systematically studies the social dimensions of fear and hope. The fluctuations of these two passions form the backdrop to his consideration of political institutions. Vacillation of mind stands to affect, he says, as doubt is related to the imagination. Indeed vacillation of mind and doubt do not differ from one another 'except in degree' (EIIIP17S). Human beings, he says in the introduction to the *Tractatus Theologico-Politicus*, are kept 'fluctuating pitiably between hope and fear' by the uncertainty of 'fortune's favours'. The fluctuations of hope and fear are mixed in with the ways in which the mind is 'swayed this way and that in times of doubt' (TTP: 3). Spinoza's treatment of mind's perturbations in 'fluctuating' and 'vacillation' are one of the many points of nexus between Spinoza's metaphysics and his insights into politics. Political institutions draw their strength from their capacity to respond to this pitiable fluctuation.

To see the significance in Spinoza's philosophy of the 'fluctuations' and 'vacillations' that arise from these powerful interactions between imagination and the emotions of fear and hope, we need to keep in mind that for Spinoza the imagination is involved in the mind's experience of both time and contingency. Time for Spinoza is a product of the imagination. *Time* here is a different concept from *duration*, which Spinoza identifies with the very existence of finite modes, in contrast with *eternity*, the very existence of Substance. Time, in contrast, involves the mind's comparisons between bodies. It is important to note here that what Spinoza calls 'duration' is ontologically grounded in the very nature of finite modes. Because imagination is involved in our awareness of finite bodies our awareness of duration is also bound up with imagination. But what Spinoza calls 'time' involves imagination in a different way. Duration is apprehended through the immediate awareness of bodies which is the very nature of the mind. Time, in contrast, is a product of imagination, dependent on the mind's capacity for comparison. We imagine time 'from the fact that we imagine some bodies to move more slowly than others or more quickly or with the same speed' (EIIP44S).

For Spinoza, then, imagination is involved in our awareness of time. But it is also involved in our awareness of contingency. There is 'in nature', he insists, nothing contingent: 'all things have been determined from the necessity of the divine nature to exist and produce an effect in a certain way' (EIP29). His treatment of the necessity of God's nature, shows, he is convinced, 'more clearly than the noon light' that there is 'absolutely nothing in things on account of which they can be called contingent' (EIP33S1). From this it may seem that the appearance of contingency is an illusion. Spinoza does indeed say that a thing is called contingent only because of a 'defect of our knowledge' (EIP33S1). But his point is not that we are mistaken in calling things contingent, but rather, as he goes on to make clear, that this is what we rightly call things when, 'because the order of causes is hidden from us', the things can never seem to us either necessary or impossible. It is where we cannot have adequate knowledge that we call things 'contingent'. But this applies generally to 'the duration of the singular things which are outside us' (EIIP31). All 'particular things' are 'contingent and corruptible'. 'For we can have no adequate knowledge of their duration ... and that is what we must understand by the contingency of things and the possibility of their corruption. ... For ... beyond that there is no contingency' (EIIP31C). It is of the nature of reason, he insists, to regard things as necessary and not as contingent (EIIP44). Our regarding things as contingent depends on the imagination (EIIP44C).

Singular things are to be called 'contingent' insofar as 'we find nothing, while we attend only to their essence, which necessarily posits their existence or which necessarily excludes it' (EIVD3). And they are to be called 'possible' insofar as 'while we attend to the causes from which they must be produced, we do not know whether those causes are determined to produce them' (EIVD4). Particular things are such that duration is their very existence; and particular things are also such that we cannot have adequate knowledge of that duration. There is 'inadequacy' here; but it does not reside in a defective knowledge of particular things; it is intrinsic to particulars as objects of knowledge. Time, in contrast to duration, is more removed from the existence of things – a product of the imagination's capacity to compare different experiences, rather than part of the very fabric of our experience of particular things.

There are different levels then of the operations of the imagination at stake in our awareness of contingency. Spinoza brings them together in an illustration describing how a child might come to experience contingency. The child who sees Peter in the morning, Paul at noon, Simon in the evening, will, when he sees Peter again, imagine the existence of Paul and of Simon with a relation to future time; and, seeing Simon in the evening, he will relate Paul and Peter to the time past, by imagining them together with past time. He will do this more uniformly, the more often he has seen them in the same order. There is here a steady expectation of the future – a lack of vacillation or fluctuating. But if it should happen that on some other evening he sees James instead of Simon, then on the following morning he will imagine, now Simon, now James together with the evening time, but not both at once. 'His imagination, therefore, will vacillate and he will imagine now this one, now that one, with the future evening time, i.e., he will regard neither of them as certainly future, but both of them as contingently future.' Similar vacillations, Spinoza observes, arise with regard to past and present (EIIP44S).

'Vacillation' and 'fluctuation' bring the operations of the imagination together with the operations of the passions. There is a close connection between the vacillation which is for Spinoza the core of contingency and the vacillations involved in the passions of fear and hope. Imagination and affect come together in the very definitions of fear and hope: both involve inconstancy with reference to ideas of future or past things whose outcome we 'to some extent doubt' (EIIIDef.Aff.XII and XIII). Neither can be experienced without the other. Where we are 'suspended in hope' we are saddened, fearing what we imagine will happen; and where we are in fear, we hope that what we hope will not take place (EIIIDef.Aff.XIIIExp).

The vacillations of imagination and the fluctuations of fear and hope are mutually reinforcing. Where events are perceived not merely as 'contingent' but also as – in a stronger way – 'possible', fear and hope are intensified. And the associative capacity of the imagination – its power to connect two external bodies by which it has been previously affected simultaneously – further complicates its interactions with the passions. 'If the mind has once been affected by two affects at once, then afterwards, when it is affected by one of them, it will also be affected by the other' (EIIIP14). The fluctuations of affect, interacting with the fluctuations of imagination, yield inevitably relations of passionate antagonism and conflict both between human beings and within individual psychic life; and the transitions between affects are exacerbated by already existing relations of sympathy or antipathy. 'From the mere fact that we imagine a thing to have some likeness to an object which usually affects the Mind with Joy or Sadness, we love it or hate it, even though that in which the thing is like the object is not the efficient cause of these affects' (EIIIP16). 'If we imagine that a thing which usually affects us with an affect of Sadness is like another which usually affects us with an equally great affect of Joy, we shall hate it and at the same time love it' (EIIIP17).

The fluctuations of mind which are intrinsic to hope and fear are compounded by the constant vulnerability of human beings to what the superstitious call 'fortune'. Returning to the preoccupations of the Balling letter, Spinoza observes that 'anything whatever can be an "accidental" cause of hope and fear; and the things which are accidental causes of hope and fear are called "good or bad omens"' (EIIIP50 and S). The operations of the passions of hope and fear are interconnected with the force of superstitions. '[W]e are so constituted by nature that we easily believe the things we hope for, but believe only with difficulty those we fear, and ... we regard them more or less highly than is just. This is the source of the Superstitions by which men are everywhere troubled' (EIIIP50S). All these complex interactions between affect and imagination remain firmly anchored in the material basis of imagination as bodily awareness.

> [T]he human Body ... is composed of a great many individuals of different natures, and so ... it can be affected in a great many different ways by one and the same body. And on the other hand, because one and the same thing can be affected in many ways, it will also be able to affect one and the same part of the body in many different ways. From this we can easily conceive that one and the same object can be the cause of many and contrary affects.
>
> (EIIIP17S)

This unavoidable materiality gives a grim realism to Spinoza's analyses of the operations of human appetites and passions – a realism which, in the final stages of the *Ethics*, however, yields an acquiescence arising from the perception of human beings as part of nature. What we are inclined to see as 'good' and 'evil' aspects of human nature are interconnected; both are grounded in the materiality of bodies and the collectivities into which they are drawn by inexorable operations of their struggle to persist. 'From the same property of human nature from which it follows that men are compassionate, it also follows that the same men are envious and ambitious' (EIIIP32S). The interactions of appetite and imagination which make this interconnection of 'good' and 'evil' unavoidable are seen, Spinoza suggests, most clearly in the unreflectively imitative behaviour of young children.

> [C]hildren, because their bodies are continually, as it were, in a state of equilibrium, laugh or cry simply because they see others laugh or cry. ... Moreover, whatever they see others do, they immediately desire to imitate it. And finally, they desire for themselves all those things by which they imagine others are pleased – because, as we have said, the images of things are the very affections of the human Body, or modes by which the human body is affected by external causes, and disposed to do this, or that.
>
> (EIIIP32S)

Spinoza's realism about the interactions of imagination and the passions involves recognition of the inevitability of hope and fear in human life. Hope and fear cannot be good of themselves. For it follows from their definitions, as we have seen, that there can be no hope without fear and fear involves sadness. Fear and hope show a defect of knowledge – a lack of power in the mind. To strive to live according to the guidance of reason is to strive to depend less on hope and to free ourselves from fear. This is Spinoza's version of 'conquering fortune' (EIVP47S). Here again there are echoes in Spinoza's philosophy of Stoic doctrine. But where the Stoics saw hope and fear as resting on false beliefs about the importance of what lies beyond human control, and freedom as residing in a retreat to reason, Spinoza's way of 'conquering fortune' rests on the use of reason to understand the operations of imagination and the passions. His version of the life of reason acknowledges the inevitability of hope and fear, along with the other passions. The power of reason resides not in shedding them but in understanding them and, to that extent, becoming free. The passivity of the passions is overcome not by

avoiding the passions but by directing on them an active understanding which remains in the realm of affect.

The interactions of affect and imagination give rise to social affinities and bonds no less than to social conflict. Fear, along with pride
and shame, brings more advantage than disadvantage. 'So since men
must sin, they ought rather to sin in that direction.' If weak-minded
men were all 'equally proud, ashamed of nothing, and afraid of
nothing', they could be neither united nor restrained by any bonds.
'The mob is terrifying, if unafraid' (EIVP54S). But Spinoza's realism
about the interactions of emotion and imagination yields also a
vulnerable optimism. The rationally schooled imagination develops its
own hopes which, although they can never be free of fear and sadness,
offer a freedom and stability that can come to have greater force than
the pitiable fluctuations of untransformed passion. In this process a
major role is played by the power, strengthened in relations of civic
friendship, to transform the illusions and superstitions of defective
imagination. All minds of necessity strive for what they conceive to be
useful to them; and because, to a mind cultivating the joys of rational
understanding nothing is more useful than similar minds, this individual striving passes naturally over into a general striving to live with
others according to the guidance of reason. This is the honourable
form of friendship which Spinoza sees as the ideal foundation of the
state. 'To man, then, there is nothing more useful than man. Man, I
say, can wish for nothing more helpful to the preservation of his being
than that all should so agree in all things that the Minds and Bodies of
all would compose, as it were, one Mind and one Body; that all should
strive together, as far as they can, to preserve their being, and that all,
together, should seek for themselves the common advantage of all'
(EIVP18S). The implications of Spinoza's way of thinking of the relations between individuals and the 'one mind and body' they can be
seen as composing, will be explored more fully in Part II. What is
important here is the bearing of these operations of imagination on
Spinoza's treatment of how the mind attains freedom and virtue.

To understand the operations of imagination and its interactions
with the emotions is to learn to replace misleading and debilitating
illusions with better fictions which enhance rather than obstruct the
activity of mind in which freedom consists. The imagination, appropriately schooled, comes to play a significant role in the critique of
socially embedded illusions and indeed in the highest exercise of philosophical thought – the mind's understanding itself as eternal – enacted
in the final sections of the *Ethics*.

Illusions and fictions

Imagination is essential to the flourishing of human beings. It is also associated with debilitating illusions. What allows Spinoza to balance out this dual stance towards imagination is his denial that the imagination is ever of itself a source of error. The role of the imagination is to confront the mind with awareness of the state of the body of which it is the idea. This bodily awareness of its nature involves awareness of the past as well as of the present and inevitably gives rise to expectations of the contingent future. The imagination of itself contains no error. Its presenting things to us as if they are present is in no way a flaw in its functioning. Error is to be understood rather as consisting in the lack of something which needs to be supplied from outside the operations of the imagination – a lack which only intellect can remedy.

Spinoza's positive stance towards the imagination is already present in his early work, *The Treatise on the Emendation of the Intellect*. There Spinoza offers an account of 'fictions' as a way of knowing half-way, as it were, between truth and falsehood. Fictitious or 'feigned' ideas are mixed methods of knowing. They partake of imagining; but, through being criticised by reason, they become a source of improved understanding. Fictions involve untruths that are knowingly entertained rather than mistaken for inadequate ideas; they are not assigned to some separate realm of non-cognitive values. They do not themselves yield adequate knowledge; but they re-work the materials of common perception, leading the mind on to a more adequate perception. Without being themselves adequate, they give access to adequate knowledge. Fictions are not true; but they are expressions of a positive mental capacity – the capacity to feign. Although it is a genuine capacity, it is one which reflects a privation. Spinoza stresses that an omniscient being would be unable to feign. We feign only where we lack knowledge – where we do not know things to be either necessary or impossible. We cannot feign either what we know to be true or what we know to be untrue. So we feign only because we are ignorant; but feigning is nonetheless a positive response to our limitations as knowers. The less the mind understands, the greater its need to resort to feigning. The less we know nature, Spinoza observes, the more easily we can feign many things, such as that trees speak, that men are changed in a moment into stones and springs, that even gods are changed into beasts and men.[9]

In taking the imagination seriously as a cognitive capacity the young Spinoza was not doing anything radically new. His immediate predecessor Descartes had, at least in his early writings, given imagination a creative role in the acquisition of scientific knowledge, crediting it with the important power of symbolising relations in ways that allow proportions to be grasped. As Dennis Sepper has summed it up in his study of Descartes's treatment of imagination, the science of nature was for Descartes at this stage not so much intrinsically mathematical as 'harmoniously proportionate'. What gives mathematics its centrality as the paradigm of knowledge is that proportion is by its nature expressible in both geometrical and arithmetical language. Imagination, understood as the faculty of grasping such relations of harmonious proportionality, is thus seen, Seppers comments, as 'the agent of intelligent perception, the foundation of physics and mathematics and the chief faculty for rising to spiritual truths' (Sepper 1996: 56–7).

This way of thinking of the role of imagination echoes ancient ideas of the cosmos as analogically structured, with the relations between different parts mirroring one another. For the young Descartes, the strength of imagination lies in its capacity to figure one kind of thing through another, manipulating representations so that one set of relations is taken as symbolising another. To allow imagination an active cognitive role in knowledge was thus not an innovation of Spinoza's mature works. What is new, however, is the emphasis on an aspect of imagination which is not primarily epistemological – its materiality. The shift, as we have seen, allows Spinoza to make the operations of imagination proper objects of the mind's rational investigation. The illusions that are inevitable when the deliverances of imagination are not 'excluded from existence' by the dynamics of intellect, now become part of the subject matter of rational inquiry. But in moving to this more ontological version of imagination, Spinoza does not abandon his older idea of the exercise of imagination as a cognitive power, an ally of reason and even one with powers which reason itself lacks. What we get in Spinoza's late writings is a conjunction of the ontological and epistemological dimensions of imagination. Imagination, rather than being just the ally of investigative reason, becomes itself the object of rational investigation. The interplay between the ontological and the epistemological – played out in the interaction between passive and active aspects of imagination – yields a Spinozistic critique of 'fictions'.

To bring out Spinoza's strategies in the critique of fictions, it is helpful to look at some of his own examples of illusions and fictions. There are unavoidable but harmless illusions which arise from bodily structure; there are also avoidable illusions through which the unenlightened are misled and coerced; finally there are the more adequate fictions through which philosophy is enabled to grasp the elusive truths of 'god, of ourselves and of things'. The two sides of Spinoza's version of imagination, arising from the equal status of mind and body as attributes of the one substance, here come into full view. Imagination reflects both the powers of body, over which the mind has no causal influence, and the powers of the mind to understand what confronts it and gain freedom through that understanding.

First the 'illusion' of the distance of the sun. When we look at the sun, Spinoza says, we imagine it to be about 200 feet away from us. This is of course an error. But the error consists not in the imagining itself but in our ignorance of the causes of the imagining. Our imagining the sun as near can coexist with our later coming to know that it is considerably further from us. The explanation of the fact that the illusory imagining can coexist with the knowledge of error is, again, the materiality of the imagination. '[W]e imagine the sun so near not because we do not know its true distance, but because an affection of our body involves the essence of the sun insofar as our body is affected by the sun' (EIIP35S). Spinoza uses the example to illustrate his thesis that error consists not in anything positive in ideas but in a 'privation of knowledge' – a privation which typically takes the form of a lack of knowledge of causes. In another example, which we will look at in detail in the next chapter, Spinoza analyses the belief in free will as another 'privation of knowledge' – 'an opinion which consists only in this, that they are conscious of their actions and ignorant of the causes by which they are determined' (EIIP35S). This illusory idea of 'free will' really consists in nothing more than ignorance of the causes of action.

Responding to a request from his correspondent Tschirnhaus for clarification of this rejection of free will, Spinoza invokes the image of a moving stone reflecting on its motion. Let us conceive, he says, of a stone which receives a certain quantity of motion from an external cause which sets it in motion. The stone's motion is compelled; that is to say, it must be defined by 'the thrust of the external cause'. Conceive now, he continues, that while the stone continues to move, it thinks, and knows that, as far as it can, it strives to continue to move. Since the stone is conscious of its striving, and not indifferent to it, it will believe itself to be free and to preserve its motion, 'for no other cause than because it wills to'. 'This', Spinoza dismissively concludes, 'is that famous human freedom which everyone brags of having, and which consists only in this, that men are conscious of their appetite and ignorant of the causes by which they are determined.'[10]

The mere knowledge of truth does not drive out the image of the sun as near; or the awareness of action which is for Spinoza all that is 'positive' in the idea of free will. For both consist in the immediate awareness of our bodies as they are affected by others – the awareness of our bodies together with others which is, as we have seen, the very nature of imagination. In this direct bodily awareness there is no room for falsity; nor is there any way in which the intellect's knowledge of the truth could of itself dispel the immediate awareness with which it coexists. This tenacity of the image in no way suggests a flaw in human nature; it just is the mind's confrontation with body – the nature of the mind as idea of body. An image understood, nonetheless, has a different place in the life of the mind from that of an image whose causes are not understood. The mind which understands the causes of its awareness of action and appetite is, as we shall see, a very different mind from one which has the awareness of action and appetite without that understanding. The lives of the wise are very different from the lives of the ignorant, although both are subject to the same necessities.

In contrast to these illusions which consist in mere privation of the understanding of causes – illusions to which the mind is subject of its nature as idea of body – there are illusions of a more complex kind which arise within the collective lives of human beings. These 'illusions of the multitude', as Spinoza sometimes calls them, are constructs around which powers and passivities – especially the passions of fear and hope – are organised. François Galichet, in an illuminating discussion of the contrast explains this second kind of illusion as a 'fiction' around which there is developed a system of connected representations, an ordering of thought through which social power is exerted (Galichet 1972). This kind of illusion is an explicit organisation of emotions, typically arising in contexts of domination and subjection. The illusion of free will here represents for Spinoza a point of nexus between those illusions which are mere 'privations' and changeable fictions which are embedded in social practices and institutions. Whereas the belief in human free will is presented as an illusion of 'privation', the belief in the divine will takes on for Spinoza a more solid status as an organising fiction – metaphorised as the 'sanctuary' of ignorance (EIApp). For Spinoza the idea of a benign or vengeful God, concerned with human wellbeing, is itself such a fiction.

The illusion of the sun as near is a direct reflection of the constitution of our bodies, and hence not readily changeable. The 'illusions of the multitude', in contrast, can be challenged by the rational mind, and replaced by alternative constructions of imagination to yield a restructuring of the representations clustered around them, and of the passions organised through them. These new fictions will themselves in turn, however, come to be embedded in frameworks of *conatus* – of desire and power which can in turn be subjected to critique. Bodies themselves, in their dynamic interactions with other bodies and their accumulated traces from those interactions, set limits to what can be changed – to what is in Spinoza's sense 'possible' as against merely 'contingent' – in the organisation of the passions. But what powers our bodies can come to have is not fixed in advance.

The critique of illusion becomes an exercise in educating our powers of imagining; and no limits can be prescribed in advance to this process. It is important to note here that for Spinoza the passage from ignorance into wisdom is not a story of 'progressive purification', in Galichet's phrase, in which the imagination is left behind. Insight into illusion is its point of departure; but the fictions of the imagination persist into the state of wisdom. The wise mind struggles to replace the illusions which block its thriving – the fictions through which those intent on domination exert power by manipulating passions of fear and hope – with new fictions which better serve the effort to persist in being, individually and collectively, as thriving unities of mind and body.

Thus in the final sections of the *Ethics*, which deal with the mind's highest achievement of wisdom, freedom and virtue, we find Spinoza consciously resorting to 'fictions'. In understanding itself through the highest form of knowledge – in relation to the idea of God – the mind still proceeds through fictions. It is through highly sophisticated exercises of imagination that we come to grasp the eternity of the mind and the intellectual love of God. To understand our eternity – which, in our less enlightened state we conceptualise through the illusion of a continued existence after death – we are to engage, Spinoza tells us, in an exercise of 'feigning'. We are to consider the mind, that is, as if it were beginning to exist, and now beginning to understand itself as eternal. Despite the contradictions which reason can discern in the exercise, it is harmless, he assures us, provided we know what we are doing. The fictions of the wise allow glimpses of the deep truths which elude reason operating without imagination. Likewise, God's self-love, the 'intellectual joy' which underpins the wise mind's own highest joy, is a 'fiction'. Strictly speaking God is incapable of either joy or love, since this would involve a transition, on the part of a supposedly perfect being, into a greater state of activity or perfection. God is really affected no more by joy than he could be affected by sadness. It is through a fiction, then, that we say that he loves either himself or us. But these fictions of the wise differ from the fictions of 'the multitude' who imagine God as a vengeful or benign ruler, and imagine their own eternity as an afterlife in which they may suffer endless torment. Spinoza's motivation in dispelling the illusion is again continuous with that of the ancient Epicureans. By losing the harmful illusion of an afterlife, the mind is released to freedom and joy in the present.

The aspirations evoked in the final stages of the *Ethics* are of a thriving individuality. But the preceding sections of the *Ethics* make it clear that these highest rational achievements are attainable only through a collective pursuit of reason. And the interconnections of the final three books of the *Ethics* with the political writings reinforce this strong orientation towards the collective dimensions of imagination. There are instructive continuities here with more modern preoccupations with the collective and anonymous operations of imagination – for example, with what has come to be called the 'social imaginary'.[11] Although this contemporary sense of the 'imaginary' is in many ways a product of modern social theory, it has continuities with the shifts in Spinoza's treatment of imagination between, on the one hand, a way of knowing and, on the other, the imagery which becomes lodged in social practices and institutional structures in ways which make it an anonymous feature of collective mental life. Spinoza's treatment of imagination moves, as we have seen, between consideration of the epistemological powers of the individual human mind, the collective interactions which strengthen those powers, and the stabilised upshots of those operations – integrated with *conatus* and with the passions – which become objects of rational understanding.

Spinoza's version of the 'imaginary' thus clearly has a social dimension. It evokes the powers and limits of human bodies in interaction. Michèle Bertrand describes it as the space where conflicts can appear – conflicts involving not only representations but also affects (Bertrand 1983: 84). Conflicts arise not only between the different affects associated with representations by different people but also within the same mind at different times. As Bertrand puts it, the imaginary occupies a middle place between 'interior isolation', in which the mind follows the course of its own idiosyncratic associational paths, and the 'total transparency' of the rational order (Bertrand 1983: 104). Because each mind is the idea of a different body, it is inevitable that there are divergent associational paths between representations. But because those different and reciprocally impinging bodies have nonetheless commonalities, there is also the possibility of communication. Intersubjectivity here rests on connections between minds which are grounded in the impinging of bodies which are both alike and different, giving rise to affects of joy and sadness, love and hate, fear and hope. Parts III and

IV of the *Ethics* map the complex interactions of imagination and affect which yield this common space of intersubjectivity, and the processes of imitation and identification between minds which make the fabric of social life.

Emotions cluster around images – traces of previous bodily modifications. The power of these images is strengthened or diminished by the dynamic social collectivities formed or disrupted by the associations our bodies form with others. In civil society the understanding of these processes is represented in laws, religious rituals and wide-ranging social fictions, which give a unity to those clustering of images and affects through which we understand – however inadequately – ourselves, others and the social wholes we form with them. The illusion of free will, resting as it does on the denial of the necessities that govern human desires and passions, is the main obstacle to the mind's entering into this collective self-understanding in which resides true freedom. Let us now see how Spinoza transforms the understanding of human freedom by attempting to dispel this powerful illusion of the imagination.

2 Spinoza's freedom

For a modern reader, what is striking about Spinoza's treatment of freedom is that it conjoins a strong affirmation of freedom with an equally strong repudiation of free will. For Spinoza the illusion of freedom does not reside in the belief that we are free, but in a distorted understanding of the nature of our freedom – in the belief that human beings are somehow exempt from the necessities that govern the rest of nature. In separating freedom from the idea of free will, Spinoza is restating and transforming an ancient ideal which locates freedom in knowledge rather than volition. To read him now is to glimpse that ancient ideal mediated through a seventeenth-century philosophy which was itself, in its time, not an expression of nostalgia for the past but a radical reformulation of the aspirations of the present. It is also to confront assumptions of modernity which have informed our own contemporary ways of thinking of freedom – assumptions which reflect theological preoccupations with divine and human will which Spinoza repudiated – and to glimpse alternatives.

Bernard Williams remarks, at the conclusion of *Shame and Necessity*, his study of the ethical ideals implicit in ancient Greek tragedy, that in our modern ethical condition, 'not only beyond Christianity, but beyond its Kantian and its Hegelian legacies', we are in important ways, in our ethical situation, 'more like human beings in antiquity than any Western people have been in the meantime' (Williams 1993: 166). Williams suggests that in attempting to bring something of those ancient ideals into modern consciousness we might 'move beyond marvelling at them, to putting them, or bits of them, to modern uses' (Williams 1993: 167). It is in that spirit that this chapter will explore the implication of Spinoza's version of freedom.

There are strong echoes in Spinoza's treatment of freedom of Stoic ideals of detachment. We are to be guided not by things outside us but rather by what our own nature, considered in itself, demands

(EIVP37S1). The ideal for Spinoza, as for the Stoics, is grounded in an understanding and acceptance of necessity. '[I]nsofar as we understand, we can want nothing except what is necessary, nor absolutely be satisfied with anything except what is true. Hence, insofar as we understand these things rightly, the striving of the better part of us agrees with the order of the whole of nature' (EIVAppXXXII). Spinoza's version gives the ideal a strong orientation towards the inherent sociability of reason – towards the ways in which individual freedom and virtue are strengthened by relations of honourable friendship, reinforced by political institutions committed to the flourishing of joyful rational affects. The ancient Stoic ideal of order is here stripped of the associations with divine will and final causes it had accrued in later theological belief. With this transformation there comes, as we will see later, also a change in the ideas of responsibility which were part of those later traditions. But to see the full significance of this shift we must first look in more detail at how Spinoza transforms the ancient Stoic connections between freedom and necessity.

Stoic images of freedom

In the thought of the ancient Stoics, not only is the belief in freedom compatible with the belief that everything happens of necessity; the acceptance and affirmation of necessity is the key to freedom. Necessity – rather than compelling us to act against our own natural inclinations – on the contrary, confirms our place in an ordered world. Freedom, as it was expressed in this ancient ideal, involved a human mind's aligning itself with this necessary order of things. Spinoza himself regarded his views as antithetical to what he saw as the core of Stoic freedom. But his treatment of freedom reiterates the close connection the Stoics saw between freedom and necessity and their emphasis on knowledge rather than the will.

In Part V of the *Ethics*, Spinoza refers dismissively to the Stoic version of freedom, which he sees as restated in the philosophy of Descartes. The Stoic alignment between rational mind and rational world, as Spinoza saw it, involved a training of the will – a forming of customs and habits, which is at odds with their alleged doctrine of the 'absolute dominion' of reason over the passions. The Stoics, he says, thought that the passions depend entirely on our will and hence that we can command them absolutely.

> But experience cries out against this, and has forced them, in spite of their principles, to confess that much practice and application

are required to restrain and moderate them. If I remember rightly, someone tried to show this by the example of two dogs, one a house dog, the other a hunting dog. For by practice he was finally able to bring it about that the house dog was accustomed to hunt, and the hunting dog to refrain from chasing hares.

(EVPref)

The Stoic metaphor of the dogs was appropriated by Descartes in his account of the control of the passions through the will in *The Passions of the Soul* (1985). In Descartes's version, a dog is 'naturally' impelled to run away when it sees a partridge 'Nevertheless, setters are commonly trained so that the sight of a partridge makes them stop, and the noise they hear afterwards, when someone fires at the bird, makes them run towards it.' Since we are thus able, with a little effort, he says, to change the movements of the brain in animals devoid of reason, it is evident that we can do so still more effectively in the case of men. 'Even those who have the weakest souls could acquire absolute mastery over all their passions if we employed sufficient ingenuity in training and guiding them' (Descartes 1985: 348). For Descartes the key to the will's control of the passions is its capacity to break up the connections through which movements of the pineal gland – the site, for Descartes, of mind's interactions with body – have been naturally joined with certain thoughts. Through changing habits, he suggests, the movements of the gland can be separated from their associations with particular passions, and new connections formed.

Spinoza dismisses this Cartesian picture of the training of the will as 'a Hypothesis more occult than any occult quality'. In Spinoza's summary, each 'will of the Mind' is united by nature to a certain fixed motion of the pineal gland; and the connection can be broken, so that through habit the motion can come to be joined to other thoughts. In attributing to the Stoics a similar ideal of controlling the passions through training the will, Spinoza is projecting back to them a concept of the will as a power of intrusion on 'natural' connections – a concept which, with hindsight, might be more plausibly seen as coming out of the intervening theological tradition based on Jewish and Christian sources.[1] But the treatment of reason's power over the passions which Spinoza goes on to develop in Part V of the *Ethics* is nonetheless in important ways a restatement of Stoic ideas. Spinoza sees the Stoic version of freedom through a frame of Cartesianism as well as intervening theological doctrines. But there are continuities between his own version of freedom as centred in the knowledge of necessity and

Stoic sources. To bring out the affinities – and the differences – it is helpful to turn to some other famous Stoic images of freedom.

In another common image used in Stoic texts, a dog tied to a cart is dragged along; if it does not want to follow, it will still be compelled to do so. 'So it is with men too: even if they do not want to, they will be compelled in any case to follow what is destined' (Long and Sedley 1987: 386). Freedom is here seen as an ideal coincidence between the dog's spontaneous movements and what the cart's movements necessitate it doing. The image is of spontaneous movement which is in fact not the determining cause of what happens. But there are puzzling things about the example. The dog would move if it were not pulled. Equally, if it is pulled, the dog will move regardless of whether it engages in spontaneous movement. Fate, we are to suppose, leads the willing and drags the unwilling. But the movements of a dog pulled 'unwillingly' will be very different – both to an external observer and from the perspective of the dog – from those of a dog which willingly follows the pulling cart, even if they both end up in the same place.

The point of the image becomes clearer when we take it in conjunction with another image which recurs in Stoic discussions of freedom – the comparison of human action to a rolling cylinder or a spinning top. An external trigger is needed to get the cylinder rolling, the top spinning. But their motion is then maintained of their own nature. The push that starts the rolling of the cylinder, the steep downward incline, without which it would not continue – these belong to 'the order, rationale and necessity of fate'.[2] There is a frame of necessities within which movement occurs. In an example cited in a fragment from Alexander's 'On Fate', a stone released from a height and not prevented cannot fail to travel downwards.[3] The falling stone moves of necessity at the time when the causes of its motion are present – a movement 'brought about by fate *through* the stone'. These necessities do not govern only inanimate things. They frame also the movement of animals in accordance with 'impulse'. Here movement is brought about by fate *through* the animal. And this 'co-fating' of animate movement sets the scene for the Stoic approach to human freedom and responsibility.

There is for the Stoics no inconsistency between necessity and responsibility. For the human mind's regulation by fate depends, as Chrysippus says, on its own 'peculiar quality'. The cylinder will not roll without external causes, but it is the nature of the cylinder itself which keeps it rolling. Likewise, for Chrysippus, although the 'order, rationale and necessity of fate' set in motion the causes of human action, the 'deliberative impulses' of our minds and our actual actions

are controlled by our own 'individual will and intellect.'[4] What origi-
nates from us is thus said to be 'co-fated along with the government of
the world'.[5] Every action in human life, says Chrysippus, is initiated by
a cause outside the acting individual and controlled solely by Fate.
This 'primary' cause, however, does not suffice to bring about the
action in a particular way that can be valued according to moral stan-
dards. The moral dimensions of the action entirely depend on the
condition of the acting individual which thus becomes a cause for
action in its own right. Like the shape of the cylinder, the moral condition of the acting individual is a 'secondary' cause. The secondary
cause is, on this Stoic model, more important than the primary cause.
But it is not conceived as outside the domain of fate. Our 'natures', no
less than the external causes of our actions, are fated. Human beings
may be dragged by fate like a dog pulled by a cart. But the locus of
freedom is not in the determining cause of the action – in the presence
or absence of an external efficient cause of the movement – but in the
human being's inner 'impulse', in the 'assent' to necessity.

On this Stoic model, necessity and responsibility, far from being
inconsistent, are interdependent. Fate is the basis of ethics – the underlying moral structure of the world.[6] By aligning our impulses with a
pre-ordained good, we achieve the only true freedom. But this alignment of individual choice with fate is cognitive rather than volitional –
an exercise, not of what we now call 'free will', but of knowledge.
Freedom resides in the acceptance and affirmation of necessity. It is
expressed through the mind's 'assent' – the 'deliberative impulse' which
expresses the nature of the mind. Cicero, reporting the view of
Chrysippus, relates the point back to the rolling cylinder model. An
'impression' encountered will 'print and, as it were, emblazon its
appearance on the mind' but assent will be in its own power; just as the
pushing of the cylinder begins its motion, but it is the cylinder's own
shape which is responsible for maintaining the motion.[7] Assent, the
mind's 'deliberative impulse', expresses the mind's own nature; and this
is where we find freedom. Epictetus talks of the 'power to use impressions' as the one thing the gods have placed in human power – the
power of 'impulse and repulsion, desire and aversion'.[8] The central
idea is that freedom resides in acting in accordance with one's 'proper
nature'. The wise will choose freely, consciously and willingly what is
ordained by Fate according to a perfectly rational order.

There are paradoxes in this Stoic ideal of living in accordance with
nature. Is the order of nature there independent of human activities?
Or does it emerge from rational choice? Julia Annas has argued that
the Stoics did not think of nature as an independent non-ethical

foundation for ethics. 'Cosmic nature' is here, she says, 'not neutral and non-ethical' (Annas 1993: 161). Spinoza's version of the ideal is more explicit about these tensions between rational activity and passive acceptance of nature. Freedom is attained, as we will see in more detail later, by transforming passivity into activity.

Stoic images of freedom reverberate in Spinoza's philosophy. His illustration of the thinking stone echoes Stoic examples of the necessities of the falling stone, the spinning top, the rolling cylinder. By inviting us to imagine the stone reflecting on its motion, Spinoza focuses attention on the immediate awareness of action which grounds the illusion of free will. Free will, Tschirnhaus had objected, surely cannot be denied without contradicting one's own consciousness. Reflecting on the immediacy of his act of writing, Tschirnhaus observes: 'I really can omit this [act of writing]. It seems impossible to deny this.'[9] Spinoza's response accepts the immediacy of the experience, but insists that this in no way contradicts the operation of external causes. Spinoza's focus is firmly on the immediacy of consciousness which Tschirnhaus sees as the strength of his case for free will – on the palpability of the introspective awareness of striving. Moving from the fantasy of conscious stones to the direct consideration of the realm of human consciousness, Spinoza suggests that the same diagnosis applies to the infant's belief that he freely wants the milk; to the angry boy's belief that he freely wants vengeance; to the timid man's desire for flight; to the drunk's belief that his loquaciousness issues from free will.[10] The belief in free will is a 'prejudice innate in all men'.[11] But Spinoza's diagnosis of this 'prejudice' takes seriously the immediacy of the experience on which it rests. The awareness of appetite or desire is not an illusion. What is illusory is the conviction that the will is something over and above this direct awareness of appetite – something which can exert a causal force which is not itself 'externally' caused.

The structure Spinoza gives for the illusion of free will is here exactly parallel to that of the illusion of the nearness of the sun, which we looked at in Chapter 1. The thinking stone's illusion consists in being aware of its movement without being aware of the external causes that determine it. The illusion of human free will likewise consists in the awareness of our own appetites in the lack of an awareness of their determining causes. But knowing that there are such external determining causes does not drive out the awareness of appetite – in Tschirnhaus's case the awareness of 'willingly' writing – any more than knowledge of the distant sun drives out awareness of the sun nearby. The knowledge of external determining causes can coexist with the immediate experience of agency.

Spinoza identifies 'impulse' with necessity, and the understanding of impulse with freedom. Having removed final causes, purposes, what remains is just the awareness of impulse as efficient cause – itself subject to other efficient causes. The awareness of impulse, in the lack of understanding of its efficient causes, is the illusion of free will. The truth of freedom, in contrast, lies in the understanding of the efficient causes of impulse. But this understanding does not remove awareness of impulse, any more than knowledge of the true distance of the sun takes away the image of it as near. So the awareness of impulse – the introspective conviction of our agency in the world – coexists with the understanding of the efficient causes of the impulse. To understand these efficient causes, in which freedom consists, is to understand the interactions of imagination and affect.

In the Stoics' use of the analogy of the rolling cylinder, as we have seen, individual nature is like the shape of the cylinder. 'External' causes are needed to get it into motion; but the 'secondary', more important, cause is the thing's own nature. In the case of human impulse, this involves for the Stoics inward 'assent' to what is necessary. So there are two different, but supposedly not inconsistent, causal stories here: the story of external causes – the push, the downward slope – and the story of the thing's nature, grasped inwardly in the case of human action as 'deliberative impulse'. The contrast echoes in Spinoza's distinction between two kinds of causal story – equally different without being inconsistent. We have, on the one hand, the relation of dependence which binds each individual necessarily to Substance as one of its modes; and, on the other, the causality of external forces which binds the individual to other finite modes. But the two kinds of dependence interlock. It is only through the mediating force of other finite modes which impinge on it that the individual has access to the sustaining power of Substance. It is only as a finite individual among other finite individuals – made vulnerable but also sustained by their collective power – that the individual exists. The shifts between the two stories enact Spinoza's treatment of the interconnections between contingency and necessity, bondage and freedom. These social dimensions of the interactions between imagination and affect are discussed especially in the last two parts of the *Ethics* and in the political writings. It is here that we see the full force and the full potential of Spinoza's version of freedom: the Stoic conjunction of freedom and necessity yields a distinctive understanding of the social dimensions of freedom.

Freedom without the will

Spinoza's version of freedom cleverly draws together concepts not commonly associated: virtue, necessity and appetite. To act well is to act from reason. But this is nothing but 'doing those things which follow from the necessity of our nature, considered in itself alone' (EIVP59D). The desire to live well is the desire to persist in existence – a desire which is 'the very essence' of a human being (EIVP18D). 'No one can desire to be blessed, to act well and to live well, unless at the same time he desires to be, to act, and to live, i.e., to actually exist' (EIVP20). But this desire for continued existence has for Spinoza a concrete immediacy which grounds our most exalted ethical aspirations in appetite. Spinoza defines desire in terms of the consciousness of appetite, which is 'the very essence of man, insofar as it is determined to do what promotes his preservation' (EIIIDef.Aff.1). All this means that the desire for virtue is closely connected with the awareness of body – 'the first thing which constitutes the actual being of a human Mind' (EIIP11) – and hence with imagination. The bodily awareness which is essential to the human mind is, as we have seen, imagination. But it is also appetitive awareness: it involves awareness of 'all the strivings of human nature that we signify by the name of appetite, will, desire, or impulse' (EIIIDef.Aff.1).

Like the Stoics, Spinoza sees the free and virtuous life as a transition from passivity to activity – in his terms, from the 'bondage' of passion to the free activity of reason. And, again like the Stoics, he sees this transition as arising not from the controlling power of a virtuous free will but from understanding alone. The key to his version of the transition is the claim that we can be 'determined by reason' to the same things by which we are 'determined by passion' (EIVP59). Wherever the passions determine us, we can instead be determined by reason. It is at first sight a mystifying claim. To understand it is to get to the heart of Spinoza's version of the power of reason and its connections with the acceptance of necessity. For Spinoza the passions are not rival forces to reason. They are not alternate sources of determination which might compete with reason for supremacy, but rather just increases or decreases in the 'power of acting' which he identifies with reason. The underlying source of our activity is always the necessity of our nature. Passions decrease that power of acting. So the transition from passions to reason is not to be construed as a shift to an alternative motivating source, but rather as the accentuation of a natural power which the passions have diminished.

In an alternative demonstration, Spinoza relates the claim to his explication of good and evil. Spinoza's treatment of good and evil in the preface to Part IV of the *Ethics* complements his repudiation of final causes in the Appendix to Part I. Human beings, he says, are accustomed to call natural things perfect or imperfect more from prejudice than from true knowledge. In the preface to Part I, he argues that we think in terms of final causes because we are conscious of our 'actions and appetites' without being conscious of their causes. He now observes that we call things imperfect not because there is something lacking in them, or because 'Nature has sinned', but rather because they do not affect our mind as much – are not as easily imagined – as those we call 'perfect'. Our unreflective notions of perfection and imperfection rest on projection from the ways things affect us. Our ideas of good and evil indicate nothing 'positive' in themselves. One and the same thing can, at the same time, be good and bad, and also indifferent. 'For example, Music is good for one who is Melancholy, bad for one who is mourning, and neither good nor bad to one who is deaf' (EIVPref).

The transitions human beings make between evil and good – between being determined by passions and being determined by reason – are thus not transitions between quite different and opposed motivating forces. We are always determined by the necessities of our natures. But these determinations can be good or evil according to whether we are affected by joy or sadness – by increases or decreases in our own 'power of acting'. If no action, considered in itself, is good or evil – if instead, one and the same action is now good, now evil, according to the affects from which it arises – it follows, Spinoza argues, that 'to the same action which is now evil, or which arises from some evil affect, we can ... be led by reason' (EIVP59D).

But does it really follow from the claim that there is no absolute good or evil that anything to which we are determined by passion can be determined also by reason? It may seem strange here that what sounds like a high-minded conclusion about the possibility of virtue should be derived from an analysis of the difference between good and evil as entirely subjective. Can the rejection of absolute good and evil facilitate transitions from passion to reason? The point becomes clearer in the light of the structural interconnections between Spinoza's versions of reason and passion. Those affects which are passions are so called because they reduce us to passivity; and they do so because the ideas of bodily transition which they incorporate are inadequate. By understanding the passions – replacing those inadequate ideas by more adequate ones – we become free. But this 'remedy' through understanding is not a shedding of affect. It is rather a restructuring of the original affect.

The Cartesian view which Spinoza ridiculed in his criticism of the dog training image in the preface to Part V presented the remedy of the passions as breaking their 'natural' connections with ideas, so that the passion comes to have different external associations – with dishonour, say, rather than safety in the case of the soldier who flees the battlefield in fear (Descartes 1985: 348, 403–4). Spinoza's remedy, in contrast, involves an internal restructuring of the affect. By understanding the passions we restructure them into rational affects. It must be particularly noted, Spinoza insists, that 'the appetite by which a man is said to act, and that by which he is said to be acted upon, are one and the same.' The difference is just the difference between an affect experienced without understanding it, and the same affect understood. All the appetites and desires, he continues, are passions only insofar as they arise from inadequate ideas, and are counted as virtues when they are aroused or generated by adequate ideas (EVP4). Thus, 'wanting others to live according to our temperament' can be either good or bad according as it involves inadequate or adequate ideas. One and the same 'appetite' will be the passion of 'ambition', which is not much different from pride in the man who is not led by reason or, on the other hand, the 'action or virtue' called 'morality', i.e., 'the desire to do good generated in us by our living according to the guidance of reason' (EIVP37S1).

What is crucial here is that understanding the operation of the causes that determine us is the source of our becoming free. Seeing through the illusions of final causes – of things happening for ends – opens up space for true understanding of the operation of efficient causes. What is called a 'final cause', a goal or purpose, is really nothing but a human appetite, considered as a 'primary cause' of something. Efficient causes are misconstrued as final causes because human beings are commonly ignorant of the causes of their appetites – ignorant of what determines them to want something. What we wrongly talk of as the 'end' for the sake of which we do something is better understood as 'appetite' – an efficient cause, which can operate either with or without our understanding its causes. So in Spinoza's version of attaining freedom the emphasis shifts to the understanding of efficient causes; and this is fundamentally a matter of understanding the interconnections and interactions of imagination and affect.

We now come to the heart of Spinoza's treatment of true freedom as arising from the understanding of the passions; and it sounds at first paradoxical. The general form of the inadequacy incorporated into the affects which are passions is thinking of things as 'free'.

> An affect towards a thing we imagine to be free is greater than that toward a thing we imagine to be necessary ... and consequently is still greater than that towards a thing we imagine as possible or contingent. ... But imagining a thing as free can be nothing but simply imagining it while we are ignorant of the causes by which it has been determined to act.
>
> (EVP5D)

Spinoza's analysis of the illusion of free will here becomes the prototype for the general condition of bondage to passion; and deliverance from that illusion becomes the prototype of freedom. Freedom fundamentally is the emergence from the illusion of freedom – that is from the illusion of free will, the ignorance of determining causes. To emerge from the inadequacy which is the mind's 'bondage' we must move from imagining things as free – i.e., simply imagining them – to understanding them in relation to their causes.

Imagination, affect and time

The connections between imagination and affect are so close, Spinoza observes, that in some contexts the two can be identified. In this treatment of the identification, we see again the crucial relations between time and imagination. Tense distinctions have an important place in Spinoza's explorations of the interactions of imagination and affect. Again there are echoes here of the Stoics. Seneca, for example, in his moral epistle on 'groundless fears' comments that even bad fortune is fickle.

> It is likely that some troubles will befall us; but it is not a present fact. How often has the unexpected happened! How often has the expected never come to pass! And even though it is ordained to be, what does it avail to run out to meet your suffering? ... Perhaps it will come, perhaps not; in the meantime it is not.
>
> (Seneca 1989: 79)

What Seneca leaves to common sense, Spinoza explains in terms of the interactions, and convergence in present awareness, of imagination and affect. The erratic fickleness of fortune is stabilised in clearer perception as the unalterable chain of causes.

The affects are for Spinoza states of awareness of bodily transitions in activity and passivity – transitions in bodily power and intensity. But because imagination involves ideas by which the mind considers a thing as present – ideas which nevertheless indicate the constitution of the human body more than the nature of the external thing – an affect is also an imagining, insofar as it indicates the constitution of the body (EIVP9D). The affects are for Spinoza transitions in bodily power and intensity. The awareness of actual bodily modification – the awareness of things as present – is fundamental to the affects; and this is what makes the definition of the affects overlap with that of imagination. All this gives a special priority to the present. But there are two ways in which the present is involved in imagination and affect: first, the awareness of the immediate state of bodily modification, which applies, by definition, to all affects and to all imaginings; and, second, the special relation to the present which arises where not only the bodily modification but its causes are present – that is, where the affect relates to something here and now, rather than past or future. Not all emotions are thus directed to the present. Some are associated with present bodily modifications which owe their causes not to something here and now but to something past which has left its trace, or to the anticipation of something future. On this contrast Spinoza bases the understanding of the interactions of imagination and affect which is crucial to reason, virtue and freedom.

An affect whose cause we imagine to be with us in the present is more intense than if we do not imagine it to be with us (EIVP9D). The images of future or past things, considered in themselves without reference to their causes, affect us just as much as if we were imagining something as present. For all are, as images, present modifications of our bodies and hence of our minds which are the 'ideas' of those bodies. The mind's capacity to have things present to it does not necessarily involve thinking of things as temporally present. But thinking of the two as coinciding – thinking of what is present to the mind as actually present in the here and now – is, as it were, a default position of the mind. The mind will posit things as actual unless something else intervenes which would lead it to 'exclude from existence' the imagined thing; so things will be regarded as actually existing or 'present' until something intervenes. The affects will be weakened when we consider as present to us other things which 'exclude' the present existence of the thing imagined.

This 'exclusion' from existence does not destroy the image, any more than true knowledge of the distance of the sun excludes the image of it as near. But in rendering the object of emotion distant from us in time

– in excluding it from present existence – our understanding of causes reduces the intensity of the image. So our imagining is affectively more intense when we imagine nothing which excludes the present existence of the external thing.

> Other things equal, the image of a future or past thing (i.e., of a thing we consider in relation to a future or past time, the present being excluded) is weaker than the image of a present thing; and consequently, an affect toward a future or past thing is milder, other things equal, than an affect towards a present thing.
>
> (EIVP9C)

This variation in intensity of the affects in relation to present, past and future shows, Spinoza claims, why human beings are not more readily moved by 'true reason' – why they yield so readily to the 'pleasures of the moment' (EIVP16 and P17S). The intensity of the present can eclipse all thought of the future. But the immediacy of the affect of joy also gives rise to the remedy of the passions and hence to freedom.

Joy involves an increase in activity – an increase in the striving to persist. Desires arising from joy will, by definition, be increased by affects of joy; while desires arising from sadness will be diminished by affects of sadness. There is in this contrast an inherent orientation of joy towards engagement with what lies beyond the self, and hence towards sociability; and there is a corresponding orientation of sadness towards disengagement and isolation. The force of a desire arising from joy will be strengthened, rather than weakened, by the power of external causes. The mind's increase of activity, which is joy, will be strengthened by its understanding the external causes of its joy. In joy, human power is strengthened by the power of the external cause; whereas the force of a desire which arises from sadness must be defined by 'human power alone' (EIVP18D). Human powers are strengthened by sharing forces with external bodies which affect us with joy. Our powers – our joys – are strengthened by 'having dealings' with things outside us; and of those external things none are more useful to us and hence more excellent than those which 'agree entirely with our nature' – our fellow human beings (EIVP18S). Our freedom is grounded in our sociability for the same reasons as our affective imaginings are grounded in our sociability. Human beings rarely live from the dictate of reason. But, Spinoza argues, it is easier to do so, and hence easier to be free in good forms of collective living than in isolation.

The social dimensions of freedom

Spinoza's version of sociability is grounded, as we have seen, in his metaphysics of individuality and in his physics of bodies. To be an individual at all is to be exposed to the external force of other bodies – to the powers, whether congenial or antagonistic – of other individuals. Since human individuals are able by virtue of their bodily complexity to imagine and remember, this intrinsic exposure to other forces – with all its possibilities of greater power and all its inherent vulnerability – means that, for them, individuality comes to involve sociability as the recognition and enactment of relations of interdependence. Wider social wholes form an economy of forces, implicated in the play of powers – of activity and passivity – which make up individual lives. These social wholes are themselves constantly broken up and transformed in the interplay of bodily powers as individuals enter into relations of activity and passivity, congeniality and antagonism. This dynamic sociability grounded in the powers of bodies is crucial, as we will see in more detail in Part II, to Spinoza's version of politics.

The inherent exposure of the Spinozistic individual to external forces raises, for modern readers, the spectre of determinism – of the subjection of individual selves to forces over which they have no control. But these external forces are also the source of the energies of the self. What may appear to be a threat to freedom is in fact the precondition of the continued existence and thriving of the self. But the idea of freedom, as we have seen, is transformed in Spinoza's philosophy into the very recognition of the power of external forces. The freedom of the individual, rather than being opposed to the power of wider social wholes, depends on the recognition of that power, without which individuality would wither away. There is an interdependence, which may appear initially paradoxical, of individual freedom and the force of social power.

In Spinoza's philosophy we see old Stoic connections between freedom and necessity take on a new social dimension. The Stoics too emphasised ideals of civic friendship. But in Spinoza's philosophy the push towards sociability comes from the very necessities of individual strivings for self-preservation. All minds of necessity strive for what they conceive to be useful to them; and because to a mind cultivating the joys of rational understanding nothing is more useful than similar minds, this individual striving passes naturally over into a general striving to live 'according to the guidance of reason'. This is the honourable form of friendship which Spinoza sees as the ideal foundation of the state.

To man ... there is nothing more useful than man. Man, I say, can wish for nothing more helpful to the preservation of his being than that all should so agree in all things that the Minds and Bodies of all would compose, as it were, one Mind and one Body; that all should strive together, as far as they can, to preserve their being, and that all, together, should seek for themselves the common advantage of all.

(EIVP18S)

Virtue and necessity here coincide. From a modern perspective, the conjunction is bound to appear paradoxical. The force of necessity seems to drive out the possibility of virtue. Spinoza brings together the language of necessary determination and the language of virtuous action: where there is necessity there is also 'right'. All, existing from the 'highest right of nature', do by that highest right those things which follow from the necessity of their own nature. If all thus lived from the 'guidance of reason', all would possess the right to preserve what they love and destroy what they hate without injury to one another (EIVP37S2). But that virtue involves acting from necessity does not mean that all are necessarily virtuous. The necessities that govern the operations of affect and imagination mean that human beings are not necessarily governed by the understanding of necessity.

Spinoza's version of freedom involves a distinctive way of thinking of the relations between reason and passions. For Spinoza, reason does not of itself have dominance over the passions, but only insofar as it involves affects – joys – which are in the rational mind more powerful than those affects which are passions. Affects can be restrained only by more powerful affects. And these restraining affects gain their strength through the sociability which is, as we have seen, inherent in affects and imagination. To understand the interactions of affect and imagination is to see that there is no real prospect of the powerful affects associated with the collective cultivation of 'honourable friendship' generally prevailing over the more negative passions that divide human beings. Society must be preserved through the manipulation of the affect of fear, so that all refrain from doing harm out of fear of greater harms.

By this law, therefore, Society can be maintained, provided it appropriates to itself the right everyone has of avenging himself, and of judging concerning good and evil. In this way, Society has the power to prescribe a common rule of life, to make laws, and to maintain them – not by reason, which cannot restrain the affects

… but by threats. This Society, maintained by laws and the power it has of preserving itself, is called a State, and those who are defended by its law, Citizens.

(EIVP37S2)

The inevitable antagonisms which arise from the divergence and discord of the passions in the state of society poses obstacles to the life of freedom and virtue which must be controlled through the imposition of external power. Because they are subject to passions which surpass their power of virtue, human beings are drawn in different directions. Reason unites them; passions divide them. But for the most part our passions are stronger than the joyful affects associated with reason. So the common good must be safeguarded by the manipulation of negative emotions: fear, humility, repentance, shame. 'The mob is terrifying, if unafraid' (EIVP54S). There is a distinctive relation here between the life of reason and the life governed by passion. Spinoza's realism about the possibilities of individual and collective virtue reflects the realism of his treatment of appetites and imagination. Pity, shame and repentance are not, for Spinoza, virtues. But they are nonetheless good, insofar as they indicate a desire to live honourably; just as pain, though never of itself good, can be said to be good insofar as it indicates that the injured part is not yet decayed. 'So though a man who is ashamed of some deed is really sad, he is still more perfect than one who is shameless, who has no desire to live honourably' (EIVP58S).

Spinoza insists that the free and virtuous life of reason draws its strength from joy rather than sadness, from generosity rather than repression. In ordering our thoughts and images, he says, we must always attend to those things which are good in each thing so that in this way we are always determined to act from an affect of joy (EVP10S). Spinoza illustrates the contrast in a discussion of different attitudes to esteem. Only the sick of mind, he says, think of the bad effects of esteem. The wise in contrast think of its good effects rather than of the evils of ambition. It is those who most desire esteem, he wryly observes, who cry out against its misuse. Just as the poor man who is also greedy will be preoccupied with talking about the misuse of money and the vices of the rich, showing that he cannot bear calmly either his own poverty or the wealth of others, so it is the 'sick of mind' who think most of the misuse and emptiness of esteem. Those who are anxious to moderate their affects and appetites from the love of freedom, in contrast, strive as far as they can to fill their minds with the gladness which arises from true knowledge of the virtues and their causes, but not at all to 'consider men's vices, or to disparage men, or to enjoy a false appearance of freedom' (EVP10S).

What emerges is an ethic centred not on praise and blame but on a realistic evaluation of what is possible for human beings – on an effort to understand how their powers can be strengthened, and on the joy which is essentially involved in the increase of those powers. To restrain the masses through the manipulation of fear and hope is very different from assisting them to be guided by reason. It is the 'superstitious', Spinoza thinks, who seek to restrain others through fear, so that they 'flee the evil rather than love virtues'. Such people, he says, aim only to make others as wretched as they themselves are; so it is no wonder that they are generally hateful (EIVP63S). 'Those who know how to find fault with men, to castigate vices rather than teach virtues, and to break men's minds rather than strengthen them – they are burdensome both to themselves and to others' (EIVAppX111). Superstition encourages us to associate good with sadness and evil with what brings joy. Only the envious take pleasure in our lack of power and misfortune. This external control exerted through the manipulation of fear and hope is only a surrogate for the true ethical life.

Those who are living the life of freedom and virtue, in contrast, hate no one, are angry with no one, scorn no one, and are not at all proud (EIVP73S). The ancient Stoics, as we have already seen, saw no inconsistency between necessity and responsibility for action. For Spinoza, too, the repudiation of free will is not seen as at odds with holding human beings responsible for what they do, or with exerting state power to suppress harmful behaviour. But, although Spinoza's philosophy echoes those ancient themes, he is not advocating a nostalgic return to past ideals. Spinoza makes of the old idea of freedom as the understanding of necessity something new which resonates not only with ideals of total knowability of nature associated with the new science but also, as we shall see in Part II, with political ideals associated with modern democracies. Ideals of responsibility take on for Spinoza a new orientation towards understanding the operations of imagination in wider collectivities, rather than towards the praise or blame of individuals. We will now see how these Spinozistic ways of thinking of good and evil, perfection and imperfection can be put to work in understanding the collective and temporal dimensions of responsibility.

3 Re-imagining responsibility

Spinoza's rejection of a free human will is framed by an equally insistent repudiation of the idea of a free divine will. Here too his philosophy can be seen as re-figuring themes from ancient Stoic thought. What emerges is the possibility of a re-conceptualising of our own contemporary ways of thinking of responsibility which may help break the grip of our preoccupation with praise and blame, while allowing us to move more constructively between ideas of individual and collective responsibility.

Providence, fate and fortune

It is crucial to the Stoic version of freedom that there is a rational frame to human life – a necessary order that is accessible to the human mind. The Stoics invoke an idea of divine will as the locus of 'providence'. But this will is not distinct from the series of causes, also identified as 'fate'. Here there is no inconsistency between providence and fate; whatever is in accordance with fate is also the product of providence. Fate, says Chrysippus in 'On Providence' is 'a certain natural everlasting ordering of the whole' so that 'one set of things follows on and succeeds another, and the interconnection is unavoidable.'[1] Fate, thus understood, is not a lack of rational order but precisely its presence – the 'rationale of the world'.[2] As Cicero says in 'On Divination', this is not the fate of superstition, but that of physics (Long and Sedley 1987: 337). The role of the sooothsayers rests on this necessity. Their predictions, says Chrysippus in 'On Fate', could not be true if all things were not embraced by fate (Long and Sedley 1987: 338).

The identification of divine will and fate – of providence and necessity – provides a setting within which it is possible to reconcile also human responsibility and the acceptance of necessity. The wise freely choose what fate demands; their choice is grounded in a totally rational order of nature, not subject to the intrusions of any divine will whose ways cannot be known. In this respect, Stoic providence is radically opposed by later Jewish and Christian insistence on the power of a divine will not itself subject to the rational order accessible to human reason. The Stoic idea of providence gives a very different frame for human freedom and responsibility from later theological ideals in which a free individual will conforms itself in obedience to the ordainings of a divine will whose reasons are inaccessible to it.

In repudiating what he saw as superstitious appeals to divine purpose as providing a context for the understanding and regulation of human action, Spinoza can again be seen as in some ways returning to these ancient ideals. But his understanding of the Stoic idea of divine providence is coloured by the intervening reconstruction of the idea in terms of a divine will that transcends the knowable rational order of the world. Spinoza brings freedom and necessity together without any framing divine purpose. His philosophy allows no notion of a 'good' that is independent of how human bodies happen to be affected by other things; for him, as we have seen, the idea of the good can be understood only through the operations of human imagination and affect. The understanding of necessity that is involved in Spinoza's version of freedom is not an 'order' created by a purposeful God whose ways remain mysterious but rather a product of the way the human body is affected by other things in the chain of determining causes.

In the Appendix to Part I of the *Ethics*, Spinoza strongly repudiates all notion of a divine will as acting for the sake of ends, and hence all notion of human life as sustained by a providence that has human interests at heart. All things, he says there, have been predetermined by God, not from freedom of will or 'absolute good pleasure', but from his 'absolute nature, or infinite power'. It is a fundamental error, he says, to think of God as acting for ends, or as having 'taken care of things' on our behalf. The belief that 'the judgments of the gods far surpass man's grasp' is for Spinoza a deep error in which superstition is rooted. God or Nature, he insists, has no 'end set before it'. All supposed 'final causes' are in fact nothing but 'human fictions'. There is perfection in Spinoza's world; but, as we have seen, it is not teleologically grounded. Indeed, to think of God as acting for ends is to deny the perfection of God – to see him as lacking something, for the sake of which he acts. To appeal to final causes in explanation is merely to express our ignorance. In freeing ourselves of the superstition of divine purpose we remove the 'foolish wonder' which makes ignorant human beings take refuge in the will of God. Divine will is for Spinoza nothing but the 'sanctuary of ignorance' to which human beings retreat when their desire for explanation of why things happen as they do drives them in a futile search for purpose.

In repudiating the belief in divine free will as a retreat to ignorance, Spinoza is seeking to resolve tensions, which had not existed in ancient philosophy, between ideas of necessity and freedom. For the Stoics divine will was not construed as disrupting the necessities of nature; it was construed rather as the order of necessary causes itself. Spinoza, in contrast, sees tensions between the idea of divine will and the necessities of nature – tensions which he resolves through repudiation of the distinction between will and understanding. Descartes had sought to resolve in a different way the tensions between Judaeo-Christian ideas of the divine will and the idea of a totally rational and hence knowable order of nature – by accepting the ultimate inscrutability of the ways of God. Descartes, however, had also been at pains to distance this metaphysical commitment to an impenetrable divine will from the concerns of scientific knowledge. God's will is so far removed from our understanding, he says in the *Principles*, that it would be arrogant to attempt to explain natural things in terms of final causes:

> When dealing with natural things we will ... never derive any explanations from the purposes which God or Nature may have had in view when creating them and we shall entirely banish from our philosophy the search for final causes. For we should not be so arrogant as to suppose that we can share in God's plans.
>
> (Descartes 1985: 202)

Rather than repudiating divine purposes, Descartes places them beyond the reach of the human mind, so that they are irrelevant to human knowledge. Final causes have no place in the operations of natural science. They do however have a place in ethical reflection. In the *Passions of the Soul*, he offers reflection on 'divine providence' as a remedy for 'vain desire'. But even here the role of the divine will echoes ancient Stoic thought more strongly than it does later Christian ideals of obedience to a causal force that surpasses human understanding. Descartes's version of providence echoes the Stoic identification of providence and fate. To reflect on divine providence is in this context to reflect on the fact that 'nothing can possibly happen other than as Providence has determined from all eternity'. 'Providence is, so to speak, a fate or immutable necessity.' Descartes is concerned to distinguish this notion of providence as necessity from the notion of 'Fortune' – a 'chimera' arising solely from errors of our intellect. In attributing what happens to 'Fortune' we regard it as contingent – as something which is not necessary but which may happen, similar things having happened at other times. But thinking of things in this way, he says, depends solely on our not knowing all the causes which contribute to each effect. If we knew all the causes, we would have no need for the concept of fortune.

> For when a thing we considered to depend on fortune does not happen, this indicates that one of the causes necessary for its production was absent, and consequently that it was absolutely impossible and that no similar thing has ever happened, i.e., nothing for the production of which a similar cause was also absent.
>
> (Descartes 1985: 389)

Descartes's idea of a divine will associated with providence is thus very different from the idea of 'fortune' as an in principle unknowable external force. We resort to 'fortune' only where we lack full knowledge of causes. Descartes's analysis of fortune is here very similar to Spinoza's later analysis of the divine will. The Cartesian divine will is not the capricious whim of a creator who disposes of things as he fancies. We must reject the 'common opinion' that there is 'Fortune' outside us which 'causes things to happen or not to happen, just as it pleases'. To say that everything that happens is 'guided by providence' is, for Descartes, as for the Stoics, not to deny but on the contrary to insist on rational order – to negate the common belief in an external 'fortune'.

> [W]e must recognize that everything is guided by divine Providence, whose eternal decree is infallible and immutable to such an extent that, except for matters it has determined to be dependent on our free will, we must consider everything that affects us to occur of necessity and as it were by fate, so that it would be wrong for us to desire things to happen in any other way.
>
> (Descartes 1985: 380)

Despite their differences, then, there is convergence between Descartes's repudiation of fortune and Spinoza's repudiation of free divine will, in relation to the scope of scientific knowledge – the grasp of the necessary chain of causes. But Descartes, in leaving space in his metaphysics for the operations of a divine will – however remote from the concerns of science – provides a very different frame for the understanding and evaluation of human action. The 'eternal decrees' of Descartes's providence leave some scope for human free will. Not everything happens of necessity. His 'remedies' for the destructive effects of 'vain desires' and the turmoil of the passions in human life is to separate out what depends on our own free will from what depends on things external to us, limiting our desires to those former things alone.

There are strong Stoic echoes in Descartes's talk of restricting our desires to what depends on us; and also in his insistence that the recognition of necessity does not involve a fatalistic quietism. For Descartes, as for the Stoics, the appropriate response to the recognition of the operations of necessity is not indifference. If there are, for example, he says, two different routes by which we might travel to a place where we have business to conduct, although Providence 'decrees' that if we go by the route we regard as safer we shall not avoid being robbed, nonetheless we should not be indifferent to which we choose.

> Reason insists that we choose the route which is usually the safer, and our desire in this case must be fulfilled when we have followed this route, whatever evil may befall us; for, since any such evil was inevitable from our point of view, we had no reason to wish to be exempt from it: we had reason only to do the best that our intellect was able to recognize, as I am supposing that we did. And it is certain that when we apply ourselves to distinguish Fatality from Fortune in this way, we easily acquire the habit of governing our desires so that their fulfillment depends only on us, making it possible for them always to give us complete satisfaction.
>
> (Descartes 1985: 381)

Both Descartes and Spinoza re-enact ancient Stoic themes. But they appropriate and change them in different ways. For Descartes the emphasis is on the proper use of individual free will, although understanding plays an important role in knowing in what circumstances the will can play a determining role. Most of our desires, he says, extend to matters which do not depend wholly on us or wholly on others, and we must therefore take care to pick out just what depends only on us, so as to limit our desire to that alone. With those things which do not depend on us, there is still room for deliberation, even though our free wills here do not play any role in determining the outcome.

As for the rest, although we must consider their outcome to be wholly fated and immutable, so as to prevent our desire from occupying itself with them, yet we must not fail to consider the reasons which make them more or less predictable, so as to use these reasons in governing our actions.

(Descartes 1985: 380)

The benign God provides for our exercise of free will. We adapt the operation of our wills to what we can control, and to those situations where there is some scope for human deliberation in how to respond to outcomes which we cannot predict, necessary though they may be in themselves. The rest we leave to providence, trusting that our fates cannot be wholly bad. For Spinoza in contrast, necessity does not come mediated through the providence of a divine purposeful will.

The crucial point here rests again on the role of imagination. Along with the notion of divine purpose, Spinoza repudiates, in the Appendix to Part I of the *Ethics*, the prevailing understanding of order. The common, reassuring conviction that there is order in things arises, he argues, from confusing the operations of imagination with those of intellect. We judge things as well or badly organised according to whether or not they are easily imagined. Human beings prefer order to confusion as if it were something more than a relation to our imagination. But our preference for 'order' over 'confusion' is grounded on nothing more than the fact that things we can readily imagine are especially pleasing to us. So to say that God has created all things in order is to misleadingly attribute imagination to God – or perhaps, Spinoza ironically adds, they see God as providing for human imagination by disposing all things so that human beings can readily imagine them.

Our errors here arise from the effacement of the reference to ourselves which is built into the very nature of imagination. The belief in final causes is a projection of the ways in which our imagination is affected by things onto the natures of the affecting things themselves. Thus, in an example, which evokes Stoic ideas of a natural harmony in things, he suggests that we wrongly take the pleasure of harmony as an expression of the natures of things, rather than of the ways in which they affect our sense organs. 'Men have been so mad as to believe that God is pleased by harmony. Indeed there are Philosophers who have persuaded themselves that the motions of the heavens produce a harmony' (EIApp). The error, as with other illusions, resides not in the imagination itself but rather in our failure to understand its operations – a failure of understanding which gives rise to scepticism when we find that what seems good to one commonly seems bad to another. But in coming to understand the operations of imagination which give rise to these different ideas of good and bad, we come, as we saw in the last chapter, to a new version of the ancient Stoic ideal of freedom as arising from the understanding of necessity. Freedom resides in understanding the interactions of imagination and affect in their individual and especially in their social dimensions.

The Appendix to Part I of the *Ethics* is a scathing attack on what Spinoza sees as a superstitious belief in providence as a sustaining framework of purpose in nature which encompasses human life. In that respect it is an attack on the legacy of Stoicism. But it can also be seen as a return to a purer form of Stoicism than the Cartesian philosophy can allow – an ideal of freedom and virtue as residing in understanding rather than will, and an affirmation of 'order' as grounded in necessity with no reference to will. But if the *Ethics* can be seen as an unflinching affirmation of necessity, it is no less true that it is a resolute engagement with the challenge of living with contingency, without retreat to any reassuring 'sanctuary of ignorance'. The underlying question with which Spinoza is engaging here is: how are human beings to live without the belief in purpose? It is the very idea of human good that is here reconstructed without reference to either the purposiveness of nature or the virtuous individual free will.

It is significant that in the course of repudiating the idea of divine purpose, in the Appendix to Part I of the *Ethics*, Spinoza repudiates also the idea of the good as anything independent of the operations of the human imagination. The idea of human good is here presented as constituted out of the interactive operations of imagination and affect. 'Order' is not created by a purposeful God whose ways remain mysterious. It is a product of the way the human body is affected by other things in the chain of determining causes. Necessity – the order of intellect – and contingency – the 'order' of imagination – are here inseparable. The fundamental concerns of the *Ethics* remain continuous with ancient Stoic concerns with how to attain tranquility in the midst of the vicissitudes of fortune. But it now has a new twist, reflecting Spinoza's treatment of the relations between imagination and intellect: how can we think necessity and contingency in such a way that we can live with both? Contingency here belongs not with intellect but with imagination. But for Spinoza, again, that is not to say that it is illusion. The real operations of imagination here reflect the unavoidable fact that human beings are part of nature.

How to think the relations between contingency and necessity – and how their integration affects how we perceive the ethical dimensions of human life – are issues that are still with us. Descartes and Spinoza engaged with the challenge of accommodating human freedom into the affirmation of necessity which promises the expansion of certainty from mathematics into the natural sciences. We now face a different challenge: how to articulate the reality of contingency, and conceptualise the ethical implications of that acknowledged contingency, in a social context where a new mastery is claimed of what was previously construed as 'fate'. But the differences between Descartes and Spinoza remain relevant.

Descartes framed the operations of individual will with his own version of providence – a frame of necessity which sets reassuring limits to human responsibility. We are still fundamentally Cartesian in the ways we think of freedom. But we have inherited his emphasis on the will without that frame of necessity as providence – the acceptance of what lies beyond our control. So we are left with a limitless sense – and expectation – of responsibility. The legacy of modernity is not so much the mastery of 'fortune' as the unthinkability of necessity in human life. For Spinoza, in contrast to Descartes, 'fortune' is the real operations of imagination and affect in human life. Freedom resides in the effort to understand these operations, changing them in the process. Fickle fortune and implacable fate both dissolve in the reintegration of reason, imagination and emotion. Reading Spinoza now can offer us the possibility of re-thinking the relations between contingency and necessity. To see more clearly how such a re-thinking can bear on issues of responsibility, we must now see how Spinoza's treatment of freedom and necessity comes together with his treatment of the relations between human individuals and collectivities.

Spinoza's 'multitude': Balibar on 'transindividuality'

Understanding individuality, within the framework of Spinoza's philosophy involves a distinctive movement of thought between a particular finite thing, the wider totality of finite modes and the power of Substance on which they all depend. For human individuality, this means a movement of thought between the individual and wider collectivities through which the power of Substance is mediated. Individual selfhood is not possible in isolation: it depends on continuing engagement with and disengagement from other selves in changing structures of affect and imagination. Selfhood arises within a complex affective framework in which emotions circulate through systems of social relations. The self's sphere of striving expands and contracts as patterns of affect, characteristically organised around images, are formed and transformed. It is especially in Spinoza's discussion of political practices and institutions in his political writings that we see the deeper conceptual implications of Spinoza's treatment of human individuality and of the relations between individuals and groups.

Etienne Balibar has drawn attention to something distinctive in Spinoza's concept of 'the multitude': when Spinoza talks of the multitude, he understands it not as the abstraction of 'the people', but as the 'historical and political reality of the mass and of crowds in movement' (Balibar 1994: 16). Imagination and affect are crucial here. The illusion of human free will is associated with imagining God as 'master', 'king' or 'legislator', demanding obedience (Balibar 1994: 10). These representations imply that humanity perceives itself as God's 'people' – a set of individuals bound together by relations of love and hate, the expectation of divine reward or vengeance. Power operates through the representations of the imagination: the masses are subjected to a monarchical political power by conferring on this power the appearance of divine right. The all-powerful God as the object of human obedience – a being imagined as 'free' – becomes the object of total obedience.

In the theory of the passions, elaborated especially in Part IV of the *Ethics*, Balibar argues, the object of analysis is not so much the individual but the form of individuality – how it is constituted, how it is preserved through composition with others, according to relations of agreement and disagreement, activity and passivity. Love and hate here become not so much relations of recognition between selves as '*concatenations of affects* which are always *partial*, which are reinforced by the repetition of encounters, by the collision of words and images, and which separate or reunite individuals in the imagination' (Balibar 1994: 27). These concatenations of affect and images are not the product of consciousness but rather produce it as 'an inadequate knowledge of our corporeal multiplicity'. Self-consciousness is inseparable from desire, joy and sadness, fear and hope. Here the constitution of individuality and the constitution of the imagining of 'the multitude' are one and the same process – fundamentally a process of imitation of affects. The object of Spinoza's concern is 'the process or the network of the circulation of affects and ideas' (Balibar 1994: 33). Relations of communication of affect between human individuals are here subsidiary to the relations of communication between the affects themselves. In this way affective communication is the very concept of 'the mass'.

Spinoza's version of democracy, on this reading, is the transformation of the circulation of affects. In his earlier book *Spinoza et la politique* (1985) Balibar uses the concept of communication to explain the nexus between the metaphysical aspects of this idea of circulating affects – its grounding in Spinoza's treatment of the powers of bodies – and its role as a political concept, giving a distinctive content to Spinoza's version of the ideal of free speech. Diversity of opinion and free communication between individuals is seen as a necessary condition of the larger social networks within which – however precariously and temporarily – the equilibrium of power is achieved. The achievement of balance, and hence stability, in the realm of politics is facilitated by the repudiation of the fiction of 'free' individuals along with the fiction of divine free will. If, as reason demands, we think of God as necessary – that is, as Nature itself in its total impersonality – fear of his 'anger' disappears. The transformed understanding of God's power brings with it a related transformation in the citizens' imagining of the power of those who govern. Rather than seeing them as all-powerful, we see them too as determined in their decisions by a general necessity. It then becomes possible for citizens to see one another – both the governed and those who govern – in relations of friendship. We become capable of loving other human beings not as creatures obeying and disobeying their creator – not as fictitiously 'free' – but as natural beings who are most useful, and hence most necessary, to us (Balibar 1985: 110).

There is an apparent paradox at the heart of Spinoza's political philosophy, which Balibar's reading highlights and attempts to resolve: a tension between his insistence on the absolute power of the State and his equally strong commitment to the freedom of the individual. On Balibar's analysis, the sovereignty of the State and individual liberty cannot be separated nor, strictly speaking, reconciled; for the contradiction lies in opposing them in the first place (Balibar 1985: 38). The key to the puzzle, he suggests, is the recognition of 'the multitude' as a third term in addition to 'the individual' and 'the State'. The individual and the State are abstractions which have sense only in relation to one another, as different modalities under which is realised the power of the multitude. Democracy, on this way of thinking of the political, involves an equilibrium of power: the forces and strivings of individuals combine to make a more powerful individual able to balance the external causes opposed to their nature (Balibar 1985: 100).

These dynamic relations between human individuals – Spinoza's version of sociability – inevitably involve negative as well as positive emotions: hate as well as love and civic friendship. The idea of antagonism is essential in Spinoza's understanding of the political; for the power of the multitude is power of discord as well as power of concord. Hate is here a form of social bond – a form of sociability. But this antagonism is not a relation of simple opposition between individual and State. The dominant and the dominated – sovereign and citizens – are equally part of 'the multitude'.

The unavoidable partiality of similitude makes ambivalence and vacillation an inextricable part of politics. Even within the same subject the operations of love and hate give rise to conflict. As Balibar, in another paper, sums up the upshot of EIIIP15–17, 'an internal conflict is generated, in which opposite affections (mainly Love and Hate) simultaneously affect the same subject with respect to the same objects' (Balibar 1997: 26). Psychic mechanisms of identification – 'affective imitation' – operate to communicate affects through the images each individual has of others who are both like and unlike themselves. The complexity of those images gives rise to ambivalence and hence to fluctuation in the affects of joy and sadness and hence love and hate and the other affects based on them. This fluctuation gives rise in turn to a fear of the difference which gives rise to it – a fear which in turn feeds into the continuing processes of communication of affect. Imagination is here a mimetic process, in which individuals associate joy or sadness with the images of other individuals, thus awakening feelings of hate and love towards them and, consequently, desires to please or displease. Complex processes of identification operate: we identify ourselves with others whom we perceive as having a partial likeness with us and we project our own affections on them. Affects are continuously circulated between individuals, reinforced and intensified through communication.

In this complex affective network the imagination of freedom plays a crucial role. Within the circulation of affects and images grounded in powers of bodies which are both similar and dissimilar to one another, isolation can only be a fiction. But the fiction of self-contained independence makes us imagine others as 'free' sources of our joys and pains. Fictions of freedom, which present it as residing in sites of independent causal force, accentuate the original passions of love or hate, making us see other individuals as specific sites of praise or blame. In Spinoza's philosophy the emphasis shifts away from praise and blame to understanding the operations of affect and imagination in which selves are multiply constituted.

On Balibar's reading 'multitude' becomes synonymous with a process of free communication between irreducible singularities. Knowledge is seen as a process of continual perfecting of communication, multiplying the power of all, and language makes a common link between the governing and the governed; there is a common usage of

words made by the 'knowers' and the 'unknowing' in communication
with one another (Balibar 1985: 116). There are contentious aspects of
Balibar's reading of Spinoza, including the apparent immediacy of the
shifts it evokes between the individual and highly structured political
organisations of power. But Balibar's analysis captures something
which is important for the potential appropriation of Spinoza's philosophy in a modern context. The circulation of affects – understanding
and transforming them, and hence understanding and transforming
what we ourselves are – becomes the central focus of responsibility.
The understanding of causal processes remains crucial. But the
concern with causes now has a different rationale. Rather than being
preoccupied with identifying individuals as sites of praise and blame,
we seek to understand the constitution of individuality – the processes
of formation of multiple identities, both individual and collective.
Understanding determining causes now has as its rationale the better
understanding of determinate content: the determinate ways in which
individuality is constituted within wider totalities of finite modes.

Determination and negation: Spinoza and Hegel

Spinoza's insights into freedom can be seen as a seventeenth-century
appropriation of Stoicism. And this philosophy in turn can be seen as
making possible, and as achieving its full expression in, Hegel's treatment of freedom. Spinoza's conviction that it is only within the
structures and practices of a social order that true freedom can be
attained is developed and transformed in Hegel's philosophy. Hegel
acknowledges his debt to Spinoza as well as his differences from him in
his *Lectures on the History of Philosophy*; but he seems not to see the
affinities between his own treatment of freedom and sociability and
Spinoza's emphasis on the interdependence and mutual vulnerability
of finite modes. Hegel's presentation of Spinoza focuses on the relations between an individual finite mode and Substance on which it
depends. What brings the two philosophies closer together is the other
side of Spinoza's analysis of the determination of finite modes: the
reciprocal relations of dependence which hold within the totality of
finite modes. For Spinoza this determination of finite modes is a
matter of determination of content as much as it is a matter of causal
relations. For him, as later for Hegel, the two senses of 'determination'
belong together. It is in the interrelations of the two senses that we see
most clearly the bearing of Spinoza's treatment of sociability on
contemporary issues of freedom and responsibility.

In his *Lectures on the History of Philosophy*, Hegel stresses the importance of a dictum – *omnis determinatio est negatio* – which he appropriates, somewhat liberally, from a letter of Spinoza's.[3] Hegel pays tribute to Spinoza's 'great proposition', allegedly enunciated there, that all determination implies negation (Hegel 1974: 285–6, see also 267). His citation of the proposition, as Macherey has pointed out, is more general than what Spinoza actually says in his letter (Macherey 1979: 158ff). In this context, Spinoza does not talk, as Hegel's paraphrase suggests, of all 'determination', but only of shape. To perceive a shape, Spinoza says, is not to perceive something as it is, but to conceive it as determined – that is to say, in as much as it is limited by another thing. Shape arises from a thing's being determined – limited – by something else.

Hegel's reflections on the theme of determination are interconnected with his discussion of Spinoza's treatment of the relations between divine freedom and necessity. For Spinoza, Hegel notes with apparent approval, God's freedom is not a matter of absolute power expressed as an 'indifferent will'. Freedom is here not expressed in a generalised, universal, all-powerful arbitrary – and hence indeterminate – will; it is expressed through God's thoughts which act as 'determinate causes'. It is in this context that Hegel sees Spinoza's alleged insistence that 'every determination is a negation' as 'specially singular' (Hegel 1974: 266–7). But it is difficult, he argues, to reconcile this insistence on determination with other aspects of Spinoza's treatment of God. God alone is Substance – positive, affirmative and consequently one; all other things are in contrast indeterminate – mere modifications of Substance, and hence nothing in and for themselves. So the connection between determination and negation, as Hegel interprets Spinoza's philosophy, has to be that everything that is 'determined' – the individual human soul included – must be a 'mere negation' (Hegel 1974: 287–8).

Spinoza's philosophy, as Hegel construes it, thus has difficulty maintaining a firm grasp of the individual, without letting it slip back into 'rigid unyielding substance'. All differences and determinations are here cast into the one Substance as into an 'abyss of annihilation'. Spinoza's Substance does not 'open itself out' into vitality, spirituality or activity. It is not yet 'spirit'. 'In it we are not at home with ourselves' (Hegel 1974: 288). Spinoza, on this Hegelian interpretation, sees determination as a falling away from reality – as a negation in which there is nothing real. Hegel presents his own system as in contrast giving reality to the negative.[4] Individuality, Hegel suggests, remains for Spinoza merely negative because here negation is not linked with self-consciousness. Spinoza's philosophy lacks the 'negative self-conscious moment' – the 'movement of knowledge', the 'moment of self-consciousness', which is the path to true consciousness of freedom (Hegel 1974: 286–7). Yet there is in Spinoza's philosophy, Hegel thinks, the beginnings of a philosophy of true individuality which finds its full expression in his own.

Hegel's critique of Spinoza thus focuses on the relation between individual mode and Substance. His complaint is that Spinoza cannot coherently articulate that relation without collapsing the infinite mode back into Substance; Substance remains undetermined, undifferentiated, while the individual mode is merely negative. But this is to miss the other dimension of Spinoza's treatment of finite modes – their mutual interaction, in which the determining force of Substance is mediated through the whole interconnected network of modes. Hegel's critique of Spinoza is oriented, as it were, to the vertical relation between Substance and individual mode, rather than to the horizontal relation in which finite modes act on and are acted on by one another. Here, along the horizontal axis of finite modes, the claim that determination involves negation can be seen not as a repudiation of finite individuals but as an insight into their interdependence. Spinoza's insight is that to be a determinate individual at all involves being causally determined by other finite things. There is no final separation possible here between an isolated individual and the wider economy of forces in which its individuality is constituted – in the case of human bodies the circulation of affects and imagination and the recognition of interdependence which is fundamental to Spinoza's notion of sociability.

The Stoic notion of freedom as the understanding of necessity runs through Hegel's reading of Spinoza and through his own philosophy. In the form in which Hegel develops the idea – most significantly in the account of freedom of the will in the *Philosophy of Right* – the necessity is articulated in terms of determinacy of content.[5] In the introduction to *The Philosophy of Right* Hegel talks of the will as containing the element of 'pure indeterminacy' – an 'unrestricted possibility of abstraction from every determinate state of mind which I may find in myself or which I may have set up in myself, my flight from every content as from a restriction' (Hegel 1979: 21–2). The two senses of determination – as causal force and as determinate content – come together here. The will in its most immediate form – the 'immediate or natural will' – is an 'immediately existing content' – 'the impulses, desires, inclinations, whereby the will finds itself determined in the course of nature' (Hegel 1979: 25).

Hegel, unlike Spinoza, keeps the idea of the will as something different from the determinations of thought. But there are strong echoes of Spinoza, and of the Stoics, in Hegel's insistence that the determinacy of 'impulse' is at odds with the idea that people most commonly have of freedom – its arbitrariness.

> If we hear it said that the definition of freedom is ability to do what we please, such an idea can only be taken to reveal an utter immaturity of thought; for it contains not even an inkling of the absolutely free will, of right, ethical life, and so forth.
>
> (Hegel 1979: 27)

Contrary to Hegel's reading, Spinoza's concern with the reciprocal causal determination between finite individuals can be seen as an affirmation of the claim that the greatest determinacy of content is the expression of the highest freedom. Let us now see how this theme bears on applying Spinoza's philosophy to the understanding of responsibility.

Spinozistic responsibility

Thinking through Spinoza's treatments of individuality and of freedom shifts attention from concern with who did what, and to what end, to seeking a better understanding of what is done and what we are who do it. It shifts our attention to the circulation of images and affects embedded in social practices. The loci of responsibility shift from individuals to social practices and institutions. But this is not just a matter of identifying new, and bigger, sites of praise and blame; it involves a re-thinking also of what is involved in the very idea of responsibility; and in how we think of the relations between individuals and groups. Responsibility and group-based identity are here transformed together. The shift can help us re-conceptualise our familiar ways of understanding identity and difference to better accommodate contemporary conditions of cultural diversity, and with it our ways of understanding what is involved in taking responsibility not only for what we do but also for what we are. Thinking Spinoza's philosophy through in our own contemporary context can help us escape some of the constraints of our usual ways of thinking of the relations between individuals and groups. The point is perhaps most helpfully expressed in spatial metaphors: Spinoza's treatment of individuality can help us to think in the space between individuals and groups – to grasp the movement of thought between the two. And, as we shall see, it can help us better understand the complexity – what

James Tully (1995) has expressed as the 'strange multiplicity' – of modern selfhood.

We have seen that for Spinoza there are collective dimensions to individual selfhood. For him there is no possibility of selfhood in isolation. To be an individual – a determinate self – at all is to be embedded in wider social wholes in which the powers of bodies are strengthened or impeded. To be an individual self is to be inserted into economies of affect and imagination which bind us to others in relations of joy and sadness, love and hate, co-operation and antagonism. But because the similitudes of bodies are partial only – because there is a multiplicity of ways in which our bodies do and do not resemble one another – there will also be a multiplicity of ways in which our individuality is constituted and maintained in the circulation and 'exchange' of affects and images. Let us now look more closely at the implications of these multiply collective dimensions of selfhood.

It has become habitual to us to think of collectivities on the model of individuals as self-contained wholes – as unitary centres of agency and responsibility. But despite the considerable attention that collective responsibility has received in recent philosophy, the philosophical imagination seems to have been strangely resistant to the impact of the idea that responsibility can be a collective matter. Indeed, in its very insistence on claims of collective responsibility, philosophical preoccupation with collective responsibility seems to have entrenched the grip of the individual as a theoretical construct. Our ways of conceptualising responsibility and agency remain fixed on the model of a self-contained individual agent, construed – either literally or, in the case of collectivities, by metaphorical extension – as site of causal agency and hence as site of praise or blame.

This apparent rigidity in our ways of imagining what is involved in bearing responsibility is striking. In trying to make sense of collective responsibility we may think of the collectivity as an over-arching super individual, whose responsibilities are not reducible to those of the individuals that compose it. Alternatively, we may think of the collectivity as a fiction – a metaphorical extension of the idea of the individual – whose responsibilities can ultimately be reduced to those of individuals. Thus, in some circumstances we hold corporations responsible for outcomes in ways that 'distribute' to the individuals that compose them; in other circumstances the collectivity itself is treated as having responsibilities that do not thus 'distribute'. Either way, our conceptualisation of responsibility remains centred on the idea of the individual as a self-contained unit which pre-exists the collectivities into which it enters.

There are important aspects of collective responsibility in the context of contemporary social conditions which are not captured through our prevailing models of self-contained individuals. The point here is not to argue against holding collectivities responsible. That is often appropriate; and the possibility of moving between the allocation of responsibility to groups and its allocation to individuals is crucial to many important issues of accountability. There are circumstances under which it is appropriate to treat collectivities as unitary entities, and hence as appropriate sites of praise and blame; and there is room for philosophical debate about what those circumstances are and how they relate to individual responsibilities. Our concern here, however, is with alternative ways of making the movement in thought between individual and collectivity – ways which might allow us to bring to reflective conceptualisation aspects of collective responsibility which otherwise remain elusive.

Imaginatively accommodating the realities of collective responsibility changes how we think of both selfhood and responsibility, allowing our preoccupations to shift away from issues of praise and blame, as well as yielding insight into less individualistic ways of thinking of selfhood. In our familiar understanding of responsibility our imagination moves from the individual to the group; we think of the group as if it were an individual. How might we think of responsibility if we allowed our imagination to move in the other direction – from the collective to the individual? Here what we have seen of Spinoza's concept of 'the multitude' – the distinctive movements of thought it makes possible between the individual and the group – may help stimulate the philosophical imagination.

Our understanding of responsibility is restrained by thinking of individuals as bordered territories, firmly separated from others in such a way that the issue of where responsibility lies is always in principle determinable. Spinoza's treatment of individuality – especially that aspect of it which Balibar terms 'transindividuality' – gives us insight into the nexus between individual and collective identity. It can help us to understand better the kinds of connection between selves which defy easy oppositions between individual and group – between self-interest and concern for the good of others. It can help us understand something which otherwise – within the restraints of our more familiar ways of thinking of selves and collectivities – can seem puzzling and inappropriate: that individuals can *take* responsibility for what they have not themselves done.

What exactly is it that is puzzling about such taking of responsibility? And what is there about it that can and cannot be accommodated within the restraints of our familiar models of self-contained individuals freely contracting into wider social entities? It is true that within the resources of those models, we can make sense of the responsibilities of a collectivity 'distributing' to the individuals that compose it. We can make sense, that is, of an individual being *held* responsible for things done by the collectivity into which she or he has freely contracted. To contract into a social group or a political party may involve a readiness to be held responsible for what it does – either because we participate in its decision-making processes or by reason of 'strict liability'. But the taking of responsibility by an individual, understood in the traditional way, makes less sense in those situations where our membership of the group is something over which we have had no control – groups into which we cannot plausibly be thought of as even implicitly 'contracting'.

Hannah Arendt has suggested that ways of thinking of responsibility which are grounded on juridical models have difficulty capturing the political dimensions of collective responsibility. Yet the term 'collective responsibility' and the problems it implies, she argues, owe their relevance and general interest to political predicaments, as distinct from legal and moral ones – political issues which should not be allowed to disappear into just a special case of matters subject to 'normal legal proceedings' or 'normal moral judgments' (Arendt 1987: 43–50). In Arendt's version of collective responsibility as a political concept, we are appropriately held responsible for things we have not ourselves done where the reason for our responsibility is our membership in a group which no voluntary act of ours can dissolve – a membership which is thus utterly unlike a business partnership which we can dissolve at will. We do not acquire such responsibilities through any decision we make as individuals or by contracting into a group whose actions or policies we thereby accept. These are responsibilities, Arendt suggests, which we have just by virtue of being who we are. We acquire them by being born into a community. This kind of responsibility, she insists, is 'always political'. It belongs to us as members of a community. We can escape it only by leaving the community; and since we cannot live without being in some community or another, this means that we can escape the responsibility only by exchanging one community for another. So the only really non-responsible people, Arendt concludes, are the outcasts – refugees, the stateless.[6]

If we think of what it is to be a self in terms of the model of self-contained individuals, freely contracting in and out of collectivities, it is difficult to understand how, simply by being born, we can acquire the burden of responsibility for past injustices in which we played no part. In *The Human Condition* (1958), Arendt invokes the Augustinian concept of 'natality' as a kind of 'second birth' – an initiation of words and deeds, 'a principle of beginning' through which we become members of a community. The beginning of an individual self as a bearer of responsibility is here construed in terms of entry into a community rather than in terms of the physical facts of birth – an initiation into language and socially meaningful action. Spinoza's treatment of individuality can offer here a way of thinking of individual selfhood which will complement the strengths and clarify the limitations of Arendt's political version of collective responsibility.

The role of imagination in Spinoza's version of individuality is crucial here. Let us now examine it more closely. Individual selfhood for Spinoza involves awareness of bodily modifications – modifications which are causally determined by the impingement of other bodies which are in consequence confusedly understood in the process of confusedly understanding our own bodies. But this bodily awareness involves not only the awareness of what is happening in the present but also the awareness of traces of past modifications – the deliverances of memory and imagination. We are aware of the determining force not only of presently acting bodies but also of those which have acted on our bodies in the past. Bodily awareness is awareness not only of the present but of the past. These determining forces, as we have seen, are sources not only of causal necessitation but also of determination in the other sense: determinacy of content; they make us the determinate individual selves that we are. The modification of our own bodies by others is constitutive of our determinate individuality, as well as causally determining what we do in the here and now. The implication of memory and imagination in these determining processes means that our past is not a shadowy unreal being of thought which we can conjure up or away at will. It is here in our present – in the modifications which stay with us in the ongoing bodily awareness which makes us what we are.

Within this complex array of bodily modifications, some relate to the impingement of other bodies here and now; others derive from past collisions and collusions of bodies. Some form the basis of collaborative relations between human individuals; others draw us into relations of conflict. Because the similitudes between bodies are partial and multiplex our awareness of other bodies and hence of our own has an inner multiplicity. Here Spinoza's version of memory and imagination can provide a frame for what can seem rigid and restrictive in Arendt's articulation of her political version of collective responsibility. Thinking through the implications of Spinoza's philosophy we can see that human bodies are not born into a single community, but into complex criss-crossing structures of reciprocal affinity – constantly formed and re-formed under the impact of rival *conatus*. It is a version of what Arendt calls 'natality' which lends itself better to the complexities of identity under contemporary conditions of cultural diversity than more unitary conceptions of cultural community. Here we get some insight into what it might be for the philosophical imagination to move from the collectivity down to the individual rather than in the other direction: the self takes on an inner multiplicity which mirrors the complex affective interaction of bodies. The complexity and multiplicity of collectivities is internalised into individual identity through the awareness of an individual body as multiply affected and modified by other bodies, the confused awareness of which is constitutive of its self-consciousness.

It is important to remember here the connections between Spinoza's version of imagination and his understanding of sociability. The awareness of human collectivities – the awareness of bodies in relation – is not a merely cognitive awareness of bodily change. It is shot through with emotion – with the awareness of bodily transition to greater or lesser states of activity. Sociability is inherently affective. The incorporation into collectivities which determines our individuality involves affective imitation – dynamic movements of emotional identification and appropriation. Even where the individual's identification with wider social wholes is largely a matter of apprehending relations in which he or she already stands – communal ties into which we are born – the identification is not a merely cognitive apprehension. Our identities are constituted through sympathetic and imaginative forming of wider wholes with others rather than through a merely cognitive grasp of pre-existing relations. Group-based identity involves self-identification; and that is a matter not only of intellect, but also of emotion and imagination. In its emphasis on the dynamic interactive movement of the bodies that make up collectivities, Spinoza's philosophy is attuned to contemporary concerns with the changing character of group-based identity under new cultural conditions.

In his book *Strange Multiplicity* (1995), James Tully describes a shift in the concept of culture under new conditions of cultural diversity. More traditional ways of understanding particular cultures as 'separate, bounded and internally uniform' have given way to a view of cultures as overlapping, interactive and internally negotiated – both internally by their members and through interaction with other cultures. The modern age is in this respect, he suggests, not so much 'multicultural' as 'intercultural'; and the most difficult thing to grasp about the new version of culture is that, as a consequence of this overlap, interaction and negotiations of cultures, the experience of cultural difference is now internal to a culture. Tully explicates the contrast in terms of spatial and visual metaphors:

> Cultural diversity is not a phenomenon of exotic and incommensurable others in distant lands and at different stages of historical development, as the old concept of culture makes it appear. No. It is here and now in every society. Citizens are members of more than one dynamic culture and the experience of 'crossing' cultures is normal activity.
>
> (Tully 1995: 11)

Cultural diversity is here seen as a 'tangled labyrinth of interweaving cultural differences *and* similarities', rather than a 'panopticon of fixed, independent and incommensurable worldviews in which we are either prisoners or cosmopolitan spectators in the central tower' (Tully 1995: 11).

Although Tully contrasts the two concepts of culture as 'old' and 'new', he does not see it as really a matter of the one replacing the other. Their coexistence, he suggests, reflects two basic human needs – two 'public goods' that are in tension under new conditions of cultural diversity and the inner multiplicity that accompanies it. On the one hand there is the critical freedom to question and challenge in practice our inherited cultural ways; on the other, the aspiration to belong to a culture and a place and so be at home in the world. There is a tension then between the need for stability and an equal need for freedom – between the need for a stable sense of identity and the need for autonomy (Tully 1995: 32). What insight can we appropriate here from Spinoza's philosophy? Within a conceptual framework which sees freedom as finding its full expression in determinacy, we can better understand the tension and its possible resolution. The tensions between Tully's two 'public goods' are resolved in practice through ongoing processes of the formation of multiple identities. Identities are constructed over time, and processes of forging identities are one and the same as the processes through which we respond to cultural diversity and the multiple possibilities for identity which they present. We resolve the tensions between freedom and stability by determining our identities – determinations which are themselves however never finally fixed, but always liable to being re-formed, re-negotiated.

In terms of Spinoza's treatment of individuality we can say that our identities are determined and re-determined through processes of emotional and imaginative identification with others, based on the relations of partial and shifting relations of similitude and dissimilitude. These identifications are built up over time and are constantly subject to changes in salience – change in what most matters to our sense of who we are. Identities involve history; but they are, as Joan Scott has put it, 'historically conferred' in ambiguous ways. Subjects are produced through multiple identifications, some of which become politically salient for a time in certain contexts. Identities are produced in an ongoing process of differentiation, constantly subject to redefinition, resistance and change (Scott 1995: 11).

Spinoza's treatment of individuality can help us see that these ongoing processes of self-identification are misconstrued if we think of them as just a cognitive identification of something already there. These multiplex identities are not independent of efforts towards self-understanding through imaginative and sympathetic identification with others. Spinoza's philosophy can help us get some insight also into the antagonistic dimensions of identity formation – into the connections between the very notion of cultural identity and notions of conflict or crisis. We will see in Part II that much of Spinoza's analysis of the interactions of imagination and affect in relations of antagonism between individual human beings can be applied, in a contemporary context, to the relations between groups – and to the internalisation of those relations within individual consciousness – in contemporary culturally diverse societies.[7]

Temporality is crucial to Tully's articulation of the 'new' concept of culture. At the most obvious level, cultural identities are formed in processes that unfold over time. But there is also a more complex involvement of time in what Tully calls the 'inner multiplicity' of selfhood under conditions of cultural diversity. It involves not only memory of what has happened, in a form in which it might be accessible to external observation; it involves also distinctive relations between imagination and time which demand a first-person perspective. Not all the things we remember as having happened in the past are things with which we now identify ourselves in the present, taking them up into a continuing trajectory of our lives. We move between present and past – selecting, bringing fragments into temporary unity. To talk of an inner multiplicity of selfhood is to evoke an open-ended range of possibilities for what a self can appropriate and enact. Some of these possibilities come from memory of direct experience in the past; others arise from imaginative appropriations from, and emotional identifications with, the powers of bodies other than our own – bodies which carry, as ours do, their pasts with them. Against the background of our understanding of what we have been in the past – which may itself of course be selectively formed – we make continuities, reaching out to future alternatives to what we have already been. Within the infinite possibilities enacted by the interactions of the totality of finite modes, identities take shape – the indeterminate becomes determinate.

All determination, as Hegel said, demands negation; and that negation can be seen in terms of limitation – the restraints of what can be imagined or felt by the individual we have been. Bodies with the powers which our bodies have – the powers they share with other bodies – may in principle have open to them the full range of possible patterns of affect and imagination that we observe in a diverse society. But our sense of our past sets limits to what can be appropriated out of that rich array of possibilities – limits to what we can make determinate. And our past is itself fluid – not just because it is open to being forgotten, misremembered and corrected; but also – and more importantly – because we can at different times appropriate to our ongoing self-identification different aspects of what we have undergone; of what continues on into our present awareness of bodily modification. Our identities become determinate through processes of sympathetic and imaginative identification which respond to our present; these responses happen in a context set by our consciousness of our past, still present to us in bodily awareness.

The ongoing forging of identities involves integrating past and present as we move into the indeterminate future; and the determining of identities is at the same time the constitution of new sites of responsibility. The processes of sympathetic and imaginative identification articulated in Spinoza's treatment of individuality and sociability create new possibilities for responsibility at the same time as they create determinate identities which are, however, inherently open to change. Thinking through issues of collective responsibility in terms of Spinoza's philosophy can help us understand how it is that individuals can take responsibility for what they have not themselves done. It can give us insight into situations where we act out of a sense of ourselves as related to others in such a way that there may be no answer to the question whether we act for ourselves or for others – out of egoism or out of altruism. Spinoza's philosophy can help us understand situations in which the taking of responsibility seems explicable only through relations of solidarity in which individuality becomes determinate through the powers exerted through wider social wholes. The fact that responsibility can be a collective matter is often explicable through the fact that the formation of selfhood is also a collective matter.

Processes of formation and transformation of individual selves inter-
weave with the assuming of responsibilities in contexts of friendship
and interdependence; and this in turn creates further possibilities of
subjectivity and agency.

Spinoza's 'transindividuality' can help us understand the temporal
dimension of collective responsibility. It can help us to understand that
responsibilities do not always rest on pre-existent identities – that they
can come into existence in the same processes as those which form
identities that did not earlier exist. The 'inner' multiplicity of cultural
identity reflects the 'external' multiplicity of the relations between
bodies. But since for Spinoza minds are just ideas of bodies the
'internal' and 'external' aspects of the multiplicity of bodily similitudes
and dissimilitudes are integrated. Our bodies retain the traces of past
modification; and those modifications in turn reflect the effects of
modifications of other bodies, in chains of causal determination going
back to the distant past. The determining of our multiple identities
involves both past and present – memory and imagination as well as
present perception. In understanding how our past continues in our
present we understand also the demands of responsibility for the past
we carry with us, the past in which our identities are formed. We are
responsible for the past not because of what we as individuals have
done, but because of what we are.

Responsibilities can be projected back into a past which itself
becomes determinate only from the perspective of what lies in the
future of that past – in our present. These temporal aspects of responsibility can be easily eclipsed in models of responsibility as resting on
clear-sighted choices of sovereign individuals with a clear understanding of who they are and of what they are doing. Spinoza's
philosophy offers a different model of selfhood which takes seriously
the temporal dimensions of human consciousness – a model which
gives salience to the multiple forming and re-forming of identities over
time and within the deliverances of memory and imagination at any
one time.

The inherent temporality of selfhood which emerges from Spinoza's
treatment of individuality is an important strand in the political
dimensions of collective responsibility. Often the political dimensions
of collective responsibility involve our taking responsibility for a past
in which we did not act – perhaps did not even exist. What our forebears did often takes in this way its determination from the future –
the future which is now our present. The retrospective determination
of what they did – from a perspective not necessarily at all available to
them – is an important part of our understanding of what we now are;

and it is our being what we now are that grounds our taking responsibility in the present, even where there is nothing for which we can be appropriately blamed.

The point of suggesting that we understand collective responsibility in terms of concepts of affect and imagination drawn from Spinoza is not that pre-existing sympathetic identifications constitute criteria for the appropriateness of attributions of collective responsibility in particular cases. The point is rather that through understanding those processes in which the taking on of responsibility is intertwined with the determining of identities, we can better understand how it is that responsibilities can be collective. Subjectivity expands when we take on such responsibilities. We become something different through the expansion of possibilities involved in a sociability which necessarily involves the past. Affect and imagination are both crucial in understanding these responsibilities and the kind of individuality in which they are caught up.

Spinoza's philosophy thus allows us to understand better some of the complexities – both for selfhood and for responsibility – which arise from the temporal aspects of selfhood – complexities which arise not from the self's relations with an external world but from its own inner relations with time. But 'inner' and 'outer' cannot here be separated in the way they might be in philosophies which see mind and body as different kinds of reality, rather than as different 'attributes' of the one reality. Spinoza's treatment of minds and bodies allows us to see that these spatial and temporal dimensions of selfhood are not sharply separated. We apprehend the present only through the modifications of our bodies under the determining power of other bodies. And the determining force of bodies on one another always reflects the ways in which both affecting and affected – modifying and modified – have themselves been affected in the past. Individual minds, as ideas of individual bodies, are ideas of other bodies too, experienced together with their own – bodies which carry the past with them in ways which make self-consciousness reach into the past no less than into what lies spatially beyond its own bodily borders.

Selfhood involves a struggle for coherence and unity. We struggle to make ourselves well-functioning temporal, no less than spatial wholes – brought together out of the rich but confusing deliverances of memory and imagination. In their relation to time, the limits of selves are less fixed than in their spatial dealings with the world. Memory and imagination may be preconditions for stable selfhood; but they are also sources of instability. The capacity to have a past and to reflect on it is crucial to selfhood; and having, in the relevant sense, a past, means that there is an internal multiplicity of selfhood – an open-ended source of possibilities for what a self can appropriate and enact. Determinacy is never gained once and for all. That it is attained at all depends on the fact that the array of possibilities for what we can be and do is subject to the limitations of, and the restraints on, the here-and-now self which interacts spatially with the world. But that here-and-now self – the self insofar as it is oriented to present and future interactions with other bodies – is also itself subject to the restraints of the temporal self – the restraints set by the determining force of all it has already been.

Selves are born into a future in which they will make individual decisions, in which they will be held responsible, praised or blamed. But they are also born into the past of communal life which both precedes and awaits them – a communal life which, under modern conditions, is not the life of one culture alone, but, in Tully's term 'inter-cultural'. Such selves have not just one but a multiplicity of pasts – pasts of collective memory and imagination which must be reckoned with in the present; and not just one 'identity', but as many as can be constructed, and carried into the future, out of this inner multiplicity. Our responsibilities, no less than our freedom, come from understanding what in this rich profusion of 'finite modes' we are – in all senses – determined to be.

Part II

Communities, difference and the present past

4   Theology, politics and norms

In the preface to Part III of the *Ethics*, Spinoza observed that most of those who have written about human passions, reason and politics have assumed that human beings follow rules and laws different from the rules and laws of nature. Such theorists have tended to conceive of human nature as transcending the rest of nature, or 'as a dominion within a dominion' (*tanquam imperium in imperio*). Those who look upon the powers and capacities of the human body with 'foolish wonder' and who assume that it is constructed 'by divine, or supernatural art' fail to understand the immanent causes through which bodies are constructed (EIApp) and therefore will be unable to understand the nature and powers of the human mind. Turning to Spinoza's theologico-political writings, an analogous claim may be found in his account of the powers and capacities of complex bodies, including bodies politic. The constitution of collective bodies, and the nature and powers possessed by such bodies, should be understood through immanent, wholly natural causes. Spinoza's insistence on analysing human nature in naturalistic terms offers an alternative perspective from which to critically reflect upon traditional notions of human nature which assume a definitive rupture between nature and political society. In traditional modern political philosophy human beings are usually understood to exit the so-called state of nature by entering contracts which mutually constrain the natural rights of each. Spinoza's political philosophy represents a critical departure both from traditional conceptions of natural right and from social contract theory.

Collective life and the theologico-political

It is highly significant that Spinoza's earliest writings in political philosophy address not only the condition and causes of political life but also the condition and causes of theological life. For Spinoza these two – politics and religion – are inevitably conjoined. Unlike philosophy, which concerns itself with reason, religion and politics are necessarily bound up with emotion, superstition and imagination. Among other things, the TTP offers an account of the origin of the Hebrew state formed by Moses after the exodus of the Jews from Egypt. Many of its pages are devoted to biblical exegesis and commentary. Perhaps contrary to expectation, it is precisely because of Spinoza's concern to analyse the particular history of the Jewish people that the TTP should be read as centrally and profoundly concerned with the political. Through a careful and detailed tracing of the peculiar travails of the Hebrews – their escape from bondage to Egypt, their consequent statelessness which Spinoza treats as returning them to a 'state of nature', and the gradual formation of themselves into a 'people' belonging to a common territory and bound by common law – the TTP aims to demonstrate the general point that all human societies and polities owe their origins to the same fundamental laws which govern all of nature. The universal condition of human beings is to be both credulous and subject to the fluctuating affects of hope and fear and this condition proves fertile ground for the flourishing of superstition. Superstition 'is engendered, preserved, and fostered by fear' and 'comes to all men naturally' (TTP: 4). Every unusual event, catastrophe, accident or reversal of fortune will be seen as 'a sign', an 'omen' or a 'portent' of the favour or disfavour of a supreme being who sits in judgement on our endeavours. Human beings come to mistake superstition for religion and thus succeed in making God or Nature appear 'as mad as themselves' (TTP: 3–4). This 'theological illusion' is natural to human life and is never completely removed, even in secular modern democratic polities (Lefort 1988). The first forms of organised authority to be recognised and respected will inevitably be based in superstition rather than reason and actually existing religions are likely to be the outcome of several, converging phenomena: the 'phantoms of imagination', genuine attempts to form rules and habits which will promote human wellbeing, as well as the cunning inventions of tyrants.

Spinoza has an ambivalent attitude towards the capacities of 'the multitude' or 'the masses' to become rational, or to pursue common goods in the absence of the threat of punishment. Those who are led entirely by passion, superstition and imagination are a volatile presence in, and danger to, the state. Fear proves to be a powerful force in holding the passions of the multitude in check. However, the masses are able to be more firmly bound to obey the sovereign power if they are motivated by love and admiration as well as by fear (TTP: 214–15; TP: 304). It is in cases such as these that the 'theological illusion' – which is universal – proves to be a powerful tool of socialisation. As Spinoza explains to his correspondent Blijenbergh, scripture speaks in stories and parables in order to be accessible to people of little learning. Rather than explaining human well-being in the language of reason, that is, in terms of cause and effect, theologians present knowledge in imaginative terms and represent God as:

> a king and lawgiver. The means [to salvation], which are nothing but causes, they called laws and wrote in the manner of laws. Salvation and destruction, which are nothing but effects which follow from the means, they represented as reward and punishment.[1]

Religion binds those under its sway through hope of finding favour quite as much as through fear of punishment. Those polities which reflect the 'positive' effects of love for, and emulation of, benevolent governors are better than, and will be stronger than, those which rely solely on fear. Fear acts to deplete rather than enhance human power because 'the greater cause of fear every individual has, the less power, and consequently, the less right, he possesses' (TP: 296). Moreover, no-one is content to be ruled by someone whom he or she considers an equal (unless it is the rule of all by all, as in democratic polities). If rulers can induce the multitude to believe that they are superior beings, or that they have a special relation with supernatural or divine forces, their rule will be more secure than it would be otherwise. Spinoza notes, apparently without disapproval, the utility of Alexander the Great's 'fiction' that his rule was divinely sanctioned:

> Alexander wished to be saluted as the son of Jupiter, *not from motives of pride but of policy*, as he showed by his answer to the invective of Hermolaus: 'It is almost laughable', said he, 'that Hermolaus asked me to contradict Jupiter, by whose oracle I am recognised. Am I responsible for the answers of the gods? It offered me the name of son: acquiescence was by no means foreign to my present designs. Would that the Indians also would believe me to be a god! Wars are carried through by prestige, *falsehoods that are believed often gain the force of truth.*' (Curtius, viii. § 8) In these few words he cleverly contrives to palm off a fiction on the ignorant, and at the same time hints at the motive for the deception.
>
> (TTP: 218, emphasis added)

Such fictions and deceptions are integral to both theological and political life and over time, as Spinoza signals, they may 'gain the force of truth'. Perhaps the novelty of the example above is that Alexander is not deceived himself; he appears not to believe in the fiction of his divinity. Often, in both theological and political life the deceiver and the deceived are not able to be separated into two groups in this fashion. Moses, for example, had just as much of an imaginative relation to God as those whom he led. The fictions which bind together communities are not always deliberately fabricated falsehoods propagated by those who stand to gain by them. Rather, social fictions may be distorted or imaginative but genuine attempts to grasp the complex relations within and between collective bodies, and between the present and the past history of those collective bodies. This is a theme to which we will return in the following chapters.

Spinoza is usually intolerant of those who, like Alexander, rule by means of Plato's 'noble lie'. In the preface to the TTP he contrasts the tyrant, who tricks his subjects by 'mask[ing] the fear which keeps them down with the specious garb of religion', with free states in which it is 'wholly repugnant' to attempt to enthral 'men's minds with prejudices, [to] forc[e] their judgement, or [to] employ any of the weapons of quasi-religious sedition' (TTP: 5). Each collective, group, people or nation, founds its identity on a distinctive history which, over time, generates distinctive social fictions. The justification for the relation of power, or governance, which holds between 'the masses' and those who govern will vary according to the nature of the identity of the group or people in question. There is not for Spinoza one atemporal 'best' form of government. While his ideal may be democracy, he is realistic about the conditions under which democratic governments may flourish. Democratic rule, which assumes a certain level of reflective knowledge in the body politic, is not a viable option for all peoples, or for one people at all times.

No-one, Spinoza observes, is born rational (TTP: 201) or born a citizen (TP: 313). The creation of viable forms of collective life, in which complex relations between many human bodies may function smoothly as the constituents of a larger body, involves a great passage of time and much trial and error. At the simplest level of human existence – whether one understands this as a 'state of nature' which actually existed, or merely as an analytic hypothesis – all will seek out that which they *imagine* will increase their powers of action and avoid that which they imagine will diminish it. And human beings are very often deceived about what will bring them joy or sadness. In his book on Spinoza's critique of religion, Leo Strauss points out that for

Spinoza 'man is inclined by nature to wishful thinking' (Strauss 1997: 219). As previous chapters have shown, three fundamental passions – desire (*cupiditas*), joy (*laetitia*) and sadness (*tristitia*) – serve as the foundation from which Spinoza derives his theory of the development of collective life. It is important to keep in mind, however, that a consideration of the political dimension of collective passions does not remove us from nature. Nature continues to be the stage on which human endeavour is played out and nature does not favour human endeavour over the endeavour of anything else to persevere in its existence. Neither does nature favour the endeavours of rational over irrational beings.

The *conatus*, or endeavour, to persevere possessed by all, is strictly equivalent to the natural right which each possesses. Spinoza's account of natural right, in other words, posits the right to do something as equivalent to having the power to do that thing. 'For instance, fishes are naturally conditioned for swimming, and the greater for devouring the less; therefore fishes enjoy the water, and the greater devour the less by sovereign natural right' (TTP: 200). Leaving aside, for the moment, the force of civil laws and conventions, the exercise of individual natural rights are not bound to consider the interests of anyone or anything apart from the interests of those who exercise them. Both the wise (who act according to reason) and the foolish (who follow passion) possess as much natural right as they have power. Moreover, in the exercise of their natural rights individuals in a state of nature 'are no more bound to live by the dictates of an enlightened mind, than a cat is bound to live by the laws of the nature of a lion' (TTP: 201). Spinoza accords no privilege to human endeavour over the endeavour of the rest of nature, and as Steven B. Smith remarks, '[t]he natural right of human beings, rather than being a mark of distinction, is no loftier or more dignified than that of fish' (Smith 1997: 124).

How and why, then, does organised human collective life arise? From where do moral rights and normative judgements come, and from what do they derive their force? We need to note that Spinoza's views on these questions are spread across the *Tractatus Theologico-Politicus*, the *Ethics* and the *Tractatus Politicus*. The picture that emerges from these texts is that Spinoza does not posit a rupture between the state of nature and political life – a rupture marked by the social contract. Political life does not, for him, transcend or supersede nature. Rather, organised forms of collective life based in agreements emerge gradually and bear the marks of the earlier theological and historical forms from which they emerged. Outside of the abstractions of political philosophy, there is no community, society or polity whose origins lie solely in contract. Human life is originally and necessarily collective life and one must look to the elements of collective life which may lead people to come to agree on appropriate constraints to the exercise of the natural rights they each individually possess. These elements are not to be found in a calculative exercise of reason but rather in the imagination, in the conative striving of each individual, to conceive and pursue what will be useful to self-preservation. Such conative striving, at least initially, predisposes human collectives to be based in the imagination and superstition, that is, in theological illusions.

The *conatus* of each dictates the pursuit of that which each judges will be useful to, and the avoidance of that which each judges will be harmful to, self-preservation. Such judgements are more likely to be based on imagination than on rational reflection. *Utility* is a central component in Spinoza's account of how and why human beings come to develop more and more institutionally structured forms of collective life. Human beings are far too frail and vulnerable to survive in nature unless they join with other human beings. And nothing, according to Spinoza, is more useful to human beings than other human beings (EIV18Siii). At the same time, nothing is more dangerous to human beings than other human beings, since 'they are more powerful, crafty, and cunning than the other animals' (TP: 296). Given that Spinoza claims 'a compact is only made valid by its utility, without which it becomes null and void' (TTP: 204), the inherent instability of human relations is unlikely to promote mutual confidence or trust. Thus, elementary collective life is unlikely to offer the freedom from fear which each desires. As Spinoza says: when natural right is exercised by each, without regard to the right of others, 'men are naturally enemies', and under these conditions, natural right exists 'in opinion rather than fact' (TP: 298).

If human collective life is to be as useful as possible to each then it must be governed by laws which each will obey. That is, all must agree to exercise their rights in a manner which does not intend to cause harm to any other member of the community. Such agreement follows from the pursuit of what each judges will promote self-preservation (including the avoidance of punishment), or an increase in power or pleasure. But once the utility of this agreement is removed, so too is the motivation for the contract. It is critical, then, that the transfer of the natural power of each to the sovereign body – whether that be a single person, a group, or the whole – results in the constitution of an *effective* power, that is, a power that no-one easily can resist. The sovereign power must be minimally capable of providing peace and security, and so freedom from fear, for all. If the sovereign power is incapable of instituting and maintaining peace, then the contract will be void. If it does not provide peace but yet retains sufficient power for many to hold it in fear, the result will be a polity which is unstable and probably tyrannical, in which case Spinoza echoes Seneca's observation that tyrants can not hold their power for very long (TTP: 206).

Many commentators have acknowledged the influence of Thomas Hobbes's thought on Spinoza's political treatises. There are many points of agreement between them about the formation of bodies politic and the rights and obligations of the subjects or citizens of such bodies (see Den Uyl 1983; Strauss 1997). There is, however, at least one crucial difference between Hobbes and Spinoza, which centres on their respective treatments of natural right. As Spinoza wrote to Jelles, the difference:

> between Hobbes and myself, consists in this, that I always preserve natural right intact, and only allot to the chief magistrates in every state a right over their subjects commensurate with the excess of their power over the power of the subjects. This is what always takes place in the state of nature.[2]

Whereas Hobbes's notion of natural right has a specifically normative dimension, Spinoza's notion of natural right does not. Hobbes's conception of natural right yields normative principles or maxims of universal significance and, consequently, the rudimentary elements of a moral philosophy (Den Uyl 1983: 10ff). Spinoza's uncompromising naturalism, on the other hand, leads him to conclude that 'the natural right of ... every individual thing, extends as far as its power' (TP: 292), and therefore, 'nothing is forbidden by the law of nature, except what is beyond everyone's power' (TP: 297). Put bluntly, the right of any given body to do as it pleases is coextensive with that body's power to do as it pleases (TTP: 246; TP: 292).

Unlike Hobbes, Spinoza does not see the sole aim of political society to be the achievement of peace and security. The true aim of government, according to Spinoza, is liberty (TTP: 259) – not merely an escape from fear or death but, more pertinently, the capacity to make use of one's life, which means for him the opportunity to develop one's powers, especially the power of reason (TP: 315–17). The agreement of all to transform their natural right into civil right effects an immanent transformation of erratic power relations into structured power relations which yield more predictable outcomes. The fluctuations between fear and hope are stabilised as many of the prior sources of fear are removed. This is the contract's utility and if the contract is ineffective the utility vanishes and those who had agreed are no longer bound by their agreement. A crucial implication of this account of contract, as involving the stabilisation of dynamic power relations, is that the contract is itself constantly being remade. The transformation of individual powers into organised, political power is not irreversible. Thus, the sovereign power is bound to act in a manner which preserves its power. In this sense, bodies politic are no different to any other thing in nature. Political powers are bound by the same law 'which bids a man in the state of nature to beware of being his own enemy, lest he should destroy himself' (TP: 312).

It may appear that for Spinoza human collective life is doomed to antagonistic relations which can only be overcome by the formation of irresistible 'blocks' of power. Such a view would be only partially correct. As we will see, in the following section, collective life opens up the possibility of forming relations based in *common notions* which, in turn, allow the development of reasonable associations. Common notions represent a more complex development of sociability in which individuals gain an understanding of what they are, what they have in common with others, and why it is in their interests to join themselves in friendship with others. The concept of common notions explains how human collective life is able to make a *qualitative* leap from relations built on hope and fear to those built on reason and fellowship. Such a leap, however, should not be seen as transcending nature but as the unfolding of nature as it is expressed through human endeavour. A proper consideration of the interpretation we offer of Spinoza's common notions will be reserved for the following section, where we will argue for the pivotal role common notions play in explicating the connection between particular modes of life and particular ways of knowing.

The sociable and mimetic nature of human passions, discussed in earlier chapters, plays a crucial part in explaining the variety of motivations for keeping contracts. Utility is central but is supported by mixed motivations of other kinds. As we have seen, the pleasures and pains of those whom we imagine to be like ourselves may easily become our pleasures and pains. Emotions are sociable and contagious. One motivation for keeping faith with others is to please them and to avoid the pain of incurring their displeasure. We possess the right, according to Spinoza, 'to act deceitfully, and to break [our] compacts, unless [we are] restrained by the hope of some greater good, or the fear of some greater evil' (TTP: 204). This greater evil is most usually understood to be fear of punishment by the more powerful sovereign. While not wishing to dispute that fear of punishment is indeed one of the great socialising forces for Spinoza, it is appropriate to stress that ostracism, being held in poor regard, or being seen as untrustworthy, may be seen by many as sufficient deterrents, or punishments, against breaking contracts. It is not only the sovereign power that may exercise the right to punish – collective conformity to social and political norms is also a powerful source for ensuring compliance. To highlight these sources of conformity has the advantage of bringing out the complexity of passions, such as fear, when they are considered in the context of *already* collective, if not strictly political, life. Such an emphasis brings out the manner in which imagination, emotion and mimetic human relations predispose human development toward structured political contexts in which the developing powers of each become entwined with, and even dependent upon, the powers of every other. On this naturalistic reading of Spinoza's social contract, the development of political and social institutions is not only gradual or incremental, it is also an ongoing and open-ended process to which all members of (especially democratic) polities, through their actions and their imaginations, contribute. This point will prove important in the following chapters which will consider both the freedoms and the responsibilities that flow from democratic political membership.

The story of 'the first man': law as command and law as knowledge

We have suggested that the TTP should be understood as more than biblical exegesis and criticism. Rather, we suggest that the TTP may be read as an exercise in theologico-political, or indeed social, criticism that in broad outline has universal significance. Likewise, Spinoza's references to the story of 'the first man' may be read as more than a critical account of Genesis and Adam's 'fall'; it may be read as an account of the condition of 'everyman'. Adam's story is an allegory of the human condition – a condition which is necessarily defined by illusions. As Deleuze points out, human consciousness itself 'is inseparable from the triple illusion that *constitutes* it, the illusion of finality, the illusion of freedom, and the theological illusion' (Deleuze 1988a: 20). Previous chapters have discussed the illusion of free will and the fiction of final causes. The story of Adam shows how these two illusions always are intertwined with the third, that is, the theological illusion.

The narrative of 'the first man' is a favourite of Spinoza's which he refers to several times: in the TTP (63–8), in the *Ethics* (EIVP68) and in his correspondence with Willem van Blijenbergh (Letters 19 and 21). Clearly, he took this story to be illustrative of the inadequacy of human self-understanding and our propensity to construct imaginative fictions about what we do not fully understand. Adam's 'sin', so the story goes, is that he freely wills his own disobedience to the free command of God not to eat of the tree of good and evil. Further, Adam interprets his fate (exile from the Garden of Eden, the necessity to toil to live and mortality) as punishment for his disobedience by a God who is angered by the transgression of his command. The story neatly encapsulates all three illusions mentioned above. Adam imagines his action is freely chosen (illusion of free will), he imagines that the world, and everything in it, was created for his ends and purposes (illusion of final causes) and he imagines that God is a being who could have willed that things be other than they are and who judges, gets angry, is forgiving – in short, who matches Adam's own self-conception in that he too possesses free will and is subject to affects (the theological illusion). Far from the first man enjoying a freedom which he knowingly abuses, Spinoza argues that Adam lacks freedom, is pitiably ignorant and powerless. He does not understand himself, God, or natural law. He is caught in a web of fictions constructed out of ignorance and superstition. Adam's error is to mistake natural law for command, a mistake that captures the essence of the 'theological illusion'. Spinoza distinguishes between natural (or divine) law and human laws or commands. It is a universal tendency for human beings to confuse natural law with decree or command and so to assume that both may be transgressed by a wicked will. But God is not a judge[3] and what Adam fails to understand is that the effect of eating the fruit follows from and depends 'necessarily on the nature of the act performed' and not 'on the will and absolute power of some potentate' (TTP: 63).

Adam's foolishness consists in supposing that things could have been otherwise and that effects would not *necessarily* follow from their causes. But this is precisely what natural law entails: effect B necessarily follows from cause A and no human – or for that matter, divine – action can make it otherwise (even God could not will that things be other than they are because God is free, according to Spinoza, only in the sense that he is unconditioned; alternatively, God acts from 'free necessity' (EIP17)). Unlike human laws or conventions, natural laws can not be broken or transgressed. Adam did not break a law and he was not the object of punishment. Rather, his state of being after eating the fruit followed necessarily from the act of eating that fruit and is entirely consistent with natural law. As Spinoza explains to

Blijenbergh, '[t]he prohibition to Adam, then, consisted only in this: God revealed to Adam that eating of that tree caused death, just as he also reveals to us through the natural intellect that *poison is deadly to us*'.[4] Hence, Adam's action is not so much wicked as stupid. His stupidity is further compounded insofar as he interprets his act and its consequences in a moral rather than a natural register. This confuses two orders: knowledge of the moral order and knowledge of the natural order. The moral order, which views the act as having evil consequences, has been confused with the natural order in which that fruit is bad *for Adam*. Neither the act nor the consequence are bad or evil in themselves. Rather, the value of the act (for Adam) lies in the relation between his body and the fruit. Neither he, nor the fruit, are 'bad' in themselves; what is bad from Adam's point of view is the effect of combining his body and the fruit.

Adam's way of knowing is thus also a way of being: the imaginative manner in which he grasps his situation is expressed through the (limited) powers he possesses. The importance of this correlation between ways of knowing and ways of being will be treated in a later section of this chapter. Here, we can note that Spinoza's reference to Adam in Part IV of the *Ethics* occurs in the context of considering freedom and the fear of death. Proposition 67 states: 'A free man thinks of nothing less than of death, and his wisdom is a meditation on life, not on death.' In the Demonstration to this proposition Spinoza considers the issue of diverse motives for action. The pertinent distinction here is between acting for the reason that one *directly* desires the outcome and acting for a reason that only *indirectly* achieves the same outcome. For example, if one obeys the laws because one reasons that such obedience promotes one's own good as well as the good of all, one would be acting directly to achieve that aim. In contrast, if the motivation for obedience to laws is fear of punishment, one's actions bear only indirectly on the outcome. Those whose motivation for action is fear express their lack of power, knowledge and virtue. Turning to Proposition 68, we can see how the distinction between direct and indirect action bears on the situation of Adam. This proposition states: 'If men were born free, they would form no concept of good and evil so long as they remained free.' Adam, as mentioned above, was not free before eating the fruit. Rather, he lacked knowledge concerning himself, God and natural law. After eating the fruit he gains an awareness of his own mortality (which he interprets as punishment) and from that point on 'rather than desiring to live' Adam comes to fear death (EIVP68). In this state of fear, Adam is particularly vulnerable to the theological illusion. In his vain attempts to decipher the illusory 'will of god', he will succeed only in making himself a home in 'the sanctuary of ignorance' (EIApp).

The story of Adam, and his inability to affirm, enjoy and make use of his life, is Spinoza's allegory for the 'savage and sad superstition' which holds that a deity would take 'pleasure in [our] lack of power', or 'ascribe to virtue our tears, sighs, fear, and other things of that kind which are signs of a weak mind' (EIVP45S). This theological illusion serves to hinder the development of those capacities which would increase our joys, our powers and our virtue. The *Ethics* may be read as an ethic of joy which acts as a counterpoint to the fearful illusions of theology unmasked in the TTP. Both the ethical and the political writings relate specific modes of life to different kinds of knowledge and varying degrees of power. Deleuze captures something important about the relation between freedom, joy and power when he writes:

> The *Ethics* judges feelings, conduct and intentions by relating them, not to transcendent values, but to modes of existence they presuppose or imply: there are things one cannot do or even say, believe, feel, think, unless one is weak, enslaved, impotent; and other things one cannot do, feel and so on, unless one is free or strong. *A method of explanation by immanent modes of existence* thus replaces the recourse to transcendent values.
>
> (Deleuze 1990: 269)

The story of the 'first man' illustrates that the source of morality, for Spinoza, is always (variable) human commands not the (invariant) laws of nature. As Macherey has argued, Spinoza's notions of natural law and right are concerned not with 'the prescriptive order of men but [with the] necessary order of things', with knowledge of laws in a physical rather than a juridical sense (Macherey 1992: 184).

Human laws set out a 'plan of life laid down by man for himself or others with a certain object' (TTP: 58). The main object is to ensure peace and security of life so that each may pursue her or his preservation, well-being and flourishing. However, because many are driven by selfishness and short-term interest, and so may be unable to appreciate the purpose of human law, legislators will frame the laws in such a way that where understanding is wanting, promised rewards and threatened punishments will guarantee compliance. In these cases, law becomes a coercive force wielded by governors over those who fall under their authority. This type of law-as-command signals a weak form of sociability where the understanding of the 'multitude' is poor and where notions of justice and virtue have little meaning. As Spinoza writes: 'a man who renders everyone their due because he fears the gallows, acts under the sway and compulsion of others, and cannot be called just' (TTP: 58). One who undertakes exactly the same actions but who understands 'the true reason for laws', does not act from compulsion and is rightly considered virtuous and just. The latter person acts directly from knowledge of the purpose of law rather than simply reacting to a command. A wise polity would frame its laws such that each, according to her or his capacity, is not prevented from exercising understanding and so is not prevented from developing the capacity to act justly and virtuously. The capacity of subjects or citizens to act from knowledge and virtue, rather than from fear of punishment, is a capacity which distinguishes those who desire to 'make use' of life from those who 'fear death'.

On Spinoza's account of human law, there are very few laws which are able to be universalised. Each people or nation has its own history, its own guiding fictions, its own idiosyncrasies which are reflected in their laws. For example, Spinoza judges the law of Moses to be specific to the Jews.

> Moses does not teach the Jews as a prophet not to kill or to steal, but gives these commandments solely as a lawgiver and judge; *he does not reason out the doctrine*, but affixes for its non-observance a penalty *which may and very properly does vary in different nations.*
> (TTP: 70, emphasis added)

It is only human laws that vary in this way and it is to human laws only that one may properly apply notions of moral normativity. What is to count as wicked, just, fair or vicious, will and does vary from community to community.

On Spinoza's view, right and wrong, justice and injustice, are terms that have reference and validity only in organised communities. '[W]rong-doing', he writes:

> cannot be conceived of, but under dominion – that is, where, by the general right of the whole dominion, it is decided what is good and what evil, and where no one does anything rightfully, save what he does in accordance with the general decree or consent.
> (TP: 298; see also TTP: 208 and EIVP37S2)

The coextension of right and power, coupled with the declaration that by power and virtue he 'understand[s] the same thing' (EIVD8), offers an indication of the degree to which Spinoza's ethics challenges the fundamental assumptions of traditional moral and political theory. As Deleuze provocatively states, '[t]he entire *Ethics* presents itself as a theory of power, in opposition to morality as a theory of obligations' (Deleuze 1988a: 104). Deleuze argues against approaching Spinoza's works through the frame of traditional moral philosophy. Such an approach will result in missing what is most contemporary, exciting and productive in the *Ethics* and the political treatises. Rather, Deleuze suggests approaching Spinoza's philosophy through an *ethological* reading which highlights the central role Spinoza gives to power relations. This reading of Spinoza departs in significant ways from traditional Spinoza interpretation. At the same time, it opens up Spinoza's thought to the present and allows us to re-conceptualise those aspects of his thought which remain compelling.

Ethological bodies

The notion of ethology is borrowed from biologists and naturalists and it considers bodies in terms of their powers and capacities for affecting and being affected. The benefit of an ethological reading of Spinoza's views on right, power, virtue and desire is that it remains faithful to Spinoza's naturalism, his 'physics of bodies', at the same time as it offers a contemporary re-conceptualisation of his metaphysics of Substance (God or Nature). Moreover, the normative principles that do emerge from an ethological approach are posterior to a range of encounters between beings – some good, some bad – which only gradually evolve into socially sanctioned normative patterns of action. Ethology describes the various powers of beings in relational terms by treating an individual as a fully integrated part of the context in which it lives and moves.

Deleuze's treatment of the notion of ethology, in the context of Spinoza's ethical and political theory, furnishes three points pertinent for our purposes. First, an ethological appraisal of any given being will attend to the materiality of existence – 'the physics of bodies' discussed in Chapter 1. An ethological appraisal will reveal what a given body seeks out and what it avoids. Thus, ethology will provide a sketch of that which aids, and that which harms, a particular being's characteristic relations with its surroundings, along with a description of its desires and aversions. Ethology eschews any analysis which seeks to determine the proper function or form of an individual by proceeding from an analysis of species, to genus, to individual. In contrast to a morality which claims to know what should count as universally good or bad, virtuous or wicked, for human beings as a 'type', ethology will not claim to know, ahead of observation and experimentation, what are the capacities of this or that being, or the powers which it may come to possess.

Second, the capacities and powers of any given body will be determined, at least in part, by the context in which it lives and moves. Powers of acting and capacities for being affected are partly determined by the circumstances in which a being finds itself. Each body exists in relations of interdependence with other bodies and these relations form a 'world' in which individuals of all kinds exchange their constitutive parts – leading to the enrichment of some and the demise of others (e.g. eating involves the destruction of one body at the same time as it involves the enhancement of the other). This relational view of power follows from the relational features of Spinozistic ontology. Chapter 3 showed how Balibar's notion of 'transindividuality' interprets Spinoza's 'physics of bodies' as generating a network of affects and images, that is, a complex system of communication between interconnected beings. Ethology, too, understands each individual as constituted within the wider totality of all other individuals and, ultimately, nature itself. The powers and capacities of an individual cannot simply be deduced from knowledge concerning the species or genus to which it belongs. The more, or less, adequate knowledge an individual has about its local and global context of existence, then the greater, or lesser, capacity that individual will have to act, rather than be acted upon. Or, what amounts to the same thing for Spinoza, that individual possesses a greater, or lesser, capacity to be virtuous.

The two points, above, refer to the agonistic relations with the rest of nature that determine the parameters of human existence – an existence that is reminiscent, or rather prescient, of Nietzsche's description of life as 'essentially appropriation, injury, overpowering of the strange and weaker ... imposition of one's own forms, incorporation' (Nietzsche 1973: 175). Spinoza is no more sentimental than Nietzsche about the general conditions of life. For example, he does not deny that (at least the higher) animals have minds and feelings but it does not follow from this that we should refrain from killing and eating them. Spinoza states: 'We have the same right against them that they have against us.' And, given that our virtue or power far exceeds theirs, this right extends to using 'them at our pleasure, and treat[ing] them as is most convenient for us' (EIVP37S1). It is a condition of human life that its endeavour to persevere in existence necessarily involves the use and, sometimes, the destruction of other bodies. This follows from the nature of the human body, which:

is composed of a great many parts of different natures, which constantly require new and varied nourishment, so that the whole Body may be equally capable of all the things which can follow from its nature, and hence, so that the mind also may be equally capable of understanding many things.

(EIVP45S)

Finally, ethology reveals the compossibility, or 'composability', of individuals whose natures agree, in at least some respects. These 'compositions' involve relations of a different order from those outlined above. Individuals who collectively combine their powers have selected out from nature that with which they may unite harmoniously, rather than engage combatively, in order to form a more extensive body with new powers. Such selections exhaust the scope of human freedom precisely because they involve becoming the cause of one's encounters with others and thus of acting rather than being acted upon. As Deleuze writes, '[i]t is no longer a matter of utilisations or captures, but of sociabilities and communities' (Deleuze 1988a: 126). The Postulates on the Body in Part II of the *Ethics* make clear that human existence, as a modal existence, cannot help but be reliant on things outside itself. Human being is not a 'dominion within a dominion' but fully part of nature and bound by its laws. If the natural right enjoyed by one individual is to avoid being cancelled out by the natural right of another then it may do so only by combining forces with individuals of the same, or similar, nature.

> [When] two individuals of entirely the same nature are joined to one another, they compose an individual twice as powerful as each one. To man, then, there is nothing more useful than man. Man, I say, can wish for nothing more helpful to the preservation of his being than that all should so agree in all things that the Minds and Bodies of all would compose, as it were, one Mind and one Body; that all should strive together, as far as they can, to preserve their being; and that all, together, should seek for themselves the common advantage of all.

(EIVP18S)

But how do human beings discover the art of composing agreeable unities? Those things which promote social cohesion are treated by Spinoza in Part IV of the *Ethics*. '[T]hings that beget harmony', he writes, 'are those which are related to justice, fairness, and being honorable.' Fear also may generate harmony but like pity, flattery and shame, it arises from weakness of mind rather than reason and these affects should be minimised in a rational polity (EIVAppXV, XVI, XXI, XXIII). The strongest and best source of harmony is a political structure which encourages an agreement in power among those who compose it.

The ideal polity, for Spinoza, is a democracy in which 'people bind themselves by those bonds most apt to make one people of them, and absolutely, to do those things which serve to strengthen friendships' (EIVApp XII). Yovel (1989b: 131) does not overstate the point when he remarks that Spinoza counters the grim Hobbesian maxim, *homo homini lupus est* (man is a wolf to man), with *homo homini deus est* (man is a God to man) (EIVP35S). It is not that Hobbes is wrong about a possible form of encounter between individuals. Rather, his account of the different orders which comprise the range of possible human compositions is incomplete. There is a 'divine' as well as a 'lupine' order and the paths from one order to the other are neither linear nor one-way. Nevertheless, the formation of harmonious complex bodies continues to present a puzzle. Given that Spinoza rejects transcendent values and final causes, what power could predispose human nature toward the formation of harmonious associations? As the last section showed, the account Spinoza offers of human passions and desire would seem to gesture toward the hopelessness of aspiring to a congenial, or reasonable, sociability.

Deleuze succinctly captures the threefold nature of the practical dilemma which confronts Spinoza's ethical and political theory. First, how does one cultivate joyful passions and freedom when 'our place in nature seems to condemn us to bad encounters and sadnesses'? Second, how are adequate ideas formed when 'our natural condition seems to condemn us to have only inadequate ideas of our body, of our mind, and of other things'? And, finally, how does one become conscious of oneself, of God and Nature when 'our consciousness seems inseparable from illusions'? (Deleuze 1988a: 28). The problem is that, on Spinoza's account, we are not born possessing knowledge about ourselves, our context, God or Nature. This knowledge must be gained through experience, by processes of trial and error, with only the passions of joy and sadness to indicate what may aid us or what may harm us. But even these joyful and sad encounters are unreliable because the same thing can be at one time a cause of joy, and at another time, a cause of sadness (EIVP33D). It is here that the ethological approach to Spinoza's ethical and political theory proves especially useful. By understanding human endeavour across time as a process of experimentation, ethology offers a 'map' or a 'code' that indicates which encounters and combinations reliably lead to human thriving, which do not, and why they do or do not. The key to the puzzle of how human beings ever come to develop their powers of reason is the idea of common notions.

The concept of common notions is introduced in Part II of the *Ethics* Propositions 37–40. The formation of these common notions is crucial to the preservation of the individual, and to the formation of reasonable relations between individuals. They are formed out of experiences of our relations with other bodies, and the joyful affects these experiences produce in us. As we have seen in earlier chapters, the passion of joy involves the 'passage from a lesser to a greater perfection', that is, it involves an increase in our force for existing, or our power to act (EIIIDef.Aff.II). The *conatus* of each (human or non-human) individual dictates that it will endeavour to seek out joyful encounters and avoid sad ones. Frequently repeated joyful encounters with another body indicates an agreement, or constructive composability between these two bodies. Repeated encounters of this kind leave traces in the body which, though initially ideas in the imagination, later become the basis for the formation of common notions. Common notions are necessarily adequate ideas and other ideas which follow from them, or may be deduced from them, are also necessarily adequate (EIIP39–40). In this way the individual begins to form knowledge of the second kind (*ratio*) as well as knowledge of the first kind (*imaginatio*). The important point to bear in mind in the context of Spinoza's political philosophy, is that these kinds of knowledge cannot be understood in purely epistemological, or cognitive terms. Rather, human knowledge is embodied knowledge and different ways of knowing always imply correlative ways of being.

In order to explain how rational collectivities are possible, an understanding of the empirical preconditions for the formation of common notions is necessary. As previous chapters have shown, human beings, like other animals, have appetites, that is, they are determined to seek out what enhances, and avoid what depletes, their powers of action. Human beings are also conscious of these appetites and capable of remembering past encounters, and so form future desires for things judged to be 'good' and aversions to things judged to be 'bad' (EIIIP9S). Human beings thus form desires to repeat those encounters which past experience has judged to be good, that is, those experiences which produced joyful passions. These empirical, or practical, preconditions – the actual joyful encounter between two bodies which have something in common – explain why an individual is drawn to, or desires, other beings with whom, in at least some respects, it agrees.

The concept of common notions does not intervene in the *Ethics* as a *deus ex machina*. Rather, that concept shows how the 'physics of bodies' and the theory of knowledge presuppose each other and work together to produce Spinoza's ethical stance. The *Ethics* presents a series of arguments against mistaking sadness and lack of power for piety or virtue. Common notions represent the hinge which connects the imagination and joyful passions to reason and adequate knowledge. Common notions arise when one body encounters another with which it is compatible and so experiences joy. Although such encounters arise through chance and so the cause of the joy will be external to the body that experiences it, the endeavour to seek out further joyful encounters will necessarily involve the endeavour to understand the cause of the joy experienced. Joyful encounters give rise to reflection upon what these two bodies have in common. If a notion can be formed of what is common between the two bodies then that notion will be an adequate idea (EIIP38; see also EVP3). So even though she or he who forms the common notion was not the cause of the joyful encounter, she or he will be the cause of the adequate idea. The formation of our initial adequate ideas, however, needs to be understood alongside the physics of bodies. Spinoza's account of the formation of common notions shows the extent to which specific modes of corporeal being and the embodied relations which determine that being imply specific modes of knowing and self-understanding. The formation of common notions is the first step on the path to becoming the active cause of one's encounters – a path that leads to understanding oneself and one's context. Deleuze identifies the importance of common notions when he writes: '[t]he description of the reasonable and free man in Part IV of the *Ethics* identifies the striving of reason with this art of organising encounters, or forming a *totality* of compatible relations' (Deleuze 1990: 262).

However, understanding how agreement between two, or more, individuals is possible represents only the beginning of a long process of experimentation, in which agreements between individuals are accompanied by quite as many disagreements. Spinoza states that '[i]nsofar as men are subject to passions, they cannot be said to agree in nature' (EIVP32), and since 'man is necessarily always subject to passions' (EIVP4C) then individuals will always disagree in some respects. All human beings can do in order to strive to preserve themselves is to form associations which will be structured such that the respects in which individuals agree outweigh the respects in which they disagree. Further, as we have seen, all associations of individuals will create 'parables', or 'social fictions', which bind each individual to the collective. At least some of these fictions will, over time, congeal into institutional forms, such as juridical norms, through which the inevitable disagreements between individuals (as members, subjects or citizens of a complex body) will be settled. Initially, however, the formation of viable associations will rely mostly upon the passions of hope and fear and will create common causes for these passions. In other words, as the previous section has shown, the simplest means for securing agreement within a collective is by creating common causes of hope of reward and fear of punishment (TP: 302). Such associations draw their force from the imagination and passions, rather than reason. Nevertheless, they may prepare for the development of reasonable associations, just as imaginative ideas may prepare the way for the formation of common notions.

As we have seen, collective or political power constrains and organises the powers of individuals from without but the introduction of common notions shows that this is not all there is to Spinoza's philosophy. The power to compose compatible relations with others, and the endeavour to harmonise our powers of composition, are capacities within each individual. Harmonious forms of sociability emerge when these two forces converge, that is, when both the powers of the individual and the powers of the collective are in harmony, they become mutually reinforcing and together constitute a well-functioning unity. Or, to take up Balibar's terminology, a democratic network of communication is created in which an equilibrium of power is achieved. This equilibrium ensures that the individual does not flourish at the expense of the community, or indeed, vice versa. We will return to this theme in the following chapter where it will be suggested that the interpretation of Spinoza's philosophy offered here may be capable of plotting a path out of the contemporary impasse between liberal individualism and communitarianism.

We have suggested that, for Spinoza, the political problem (how do we come to form reasonable collectivities?) is analogous to the epistemological problem (how do we come to form adequate ideas?). This interpretation has the virtue of bringing together particular ways of knowing with corresponding ways of life. It brings out the potential of Spinoza's philosophy to articulate an embodied ethical and political theory appropriate to different kinds of individuals, the different kinds of polities in which they dwell, and the different modalities of self-understanding which they express; and it does so without recourse to transcendent, universal norms by which to judge such individuals, associations and understandings. This is not to say, however, that one cannot make judgements or comparisons at all. However, such evaluations will be based on immanent norms and on the virtue or power of an individual, or community of individuals. Ethology thus proffers a means of extrapolating from Spinoza's philosophy and a means of studying difference that does not involve a hierarchical or judgemental moralism. Rather, it suggests that the specific power of human being is the 'art' of creating or 'selecting' harmonious unities through which the powers of individuals may be enhanced. The forms that such communities may take will vary from one place to the next, and from one time to another.

In a manner that again parallels Nietzschean philosophy, Spinoza's political theory may be seen to offer 'a genealogy of the passions of the social body' (Hardt 1995: 26). The theologies, moralities and imaginaries of various forms of sociability thus offer a record, of sorts, of the development and history of this or that complex body. Indeed, as shown above, the TTP may be read as a genealogical account of the formation of the Jewish people. Perhaps unlike Nietzsche, our reading of Spinoza's philosophy may be seen to provide not simply an account of how a people came to be who they are (a genealogy of Judaism) but also an account which offers, given a knowledge of that genealogy, what a people may become through gaining a reflective knowledge of their capacities. Spinoza's ethical and political writings, in other words, may be seen to suggest both a method of understanding what one is on the basis of one's past (genealogy) *and* a knowledge of what one may become on a basis of an increase in the knowledge of one's powers and capacities (ethology). As later chapters will argue, this approach aims to provide conceptual tools for critical reflection on the freedoms we enjoy and on the responsibilities we bear in the present. We argue that such a view, far from leading to moral nihilism or relativism, furnishes a particularly robust notion of responsibility.

Power, politics and norms

Douglas Den Uyl has rightly argued that 'one must think of Spinoza's political theory as an unfolding of the implications of equating right with power' (Den Uyl 1983: 19). Along with Deleuze, Den Uyl maintains that 'Spinoza's political philosophy is a philosophy of power' (Den Uyl 1983: 97). The notion of ethology has been helpful in drawing out the centrality of the affects both to Spinoza's understanding of power and his account of the development of human sociability. Moreover, the analysis it provides treats natural right without reference to transcendent norms. However, if natural right does not yield normative judgements concerning types of individual and types of sociability, how may a Spinozist political theorist condemn vicious acts or tyrannical governments? Both Spinoza's contemporaries, and Spinoza scholars today, recoil from this apparently unavoidable conclusion.

Edwin Curley, for example, wonders if 'viewing things *sub specie aeternitatis* requires us to accept the success of [tyrannical] governments so long as they are able to maintain their power?' and '[i]f so, does being a good Spinozist not require a level of detachment from individual human suffering which is either superhuman or subhuman?' (Curley 1996: 334). Curley argues that Spinoza's notion of natural right as coextensive with power limits, or 'handicaps', one's ability to condemn or criticise tyrannies. The lack of normative content in Spinoza's philosophy of natural right, he concludes, is 'a defect in his political philosophy' (Curley 1996: 335). Curley, and others, are concerned with what may be called, in the most general terms, the problem of evil and the apportioning of responsibility. More particularly, he is worried that a philosophy of immanence, which equates God and Nature, and right and power, is incapable of making effective moral judgements. The virtually synonymous meaning of right, power and virtue in Spinoza's philosophy does indeed render problematic the basis upon which a tradition of critical philosophy has developed. However, we maintain that the reading of Spinoza's philosophy offered here is capable of providing an alternative critical perspective on political and ethical life.

Thanks to the persistence of Spinoza's correspondent, Blijenbergh, there are several letters which lay out in detail Spinoza's own response to the problem of evil. Blijenbergh's question to Spinoza captures the essence of our dilemma. He asks: 'if there was a mind to whose singular nature the pursuit of sensual pleasure or knavery was not contrary, is there a reason for virtue which would have to move it to do good and omit evil?'[5] Spinoza responds that the question 'presupposes a contradiction'.

> It is as if someone were to ask: if it agreed better with the nature of someone to hang himself, would there be reasons why he should not hang himself? But suppose it were possible that there should be such a nature. Then I say (whether I grant free will or not) that if anyone sees that he can live better on the gallows than at his table, he would act very foolishly if he did not go hang himself. One who saw clearly that in fact he would enjoy a better and more perfect life or essence by being a knave than by following virtue would also be a fool if he were not a knave. For

acts of knavery would be virtue in relation to such a perverted human nature.[6]

Spinoza is not suggesting that such a perverse individual does, or could, exist. Rather, he argues by *reductio ad absurdum* against Blijenbergh's position which – like the story of the first man – confuses the two orders of human existence: the natural and the moral. Natural laws cannot be broken or disobeyed. Human power in relation to natural laws is limited to its striving to understand them. It is only socio-political laws, developed through a long process of human experimentation, and selected for their ability to promote human survival, that are violable. Blijenbergh's question rests upon a theological rather than a philosophical understanding of virtue and vice, good and evil. As we have seen, theology typically inverts the actual order of causes and effects. Theological accounts of good and evil, sin and redemption, do sometimes contain in distorted form elements of truth. In some contexts, they may be understood as useful fictions or 'parables' which attempt to convey knowledge about the world through the imagination. In other contexts, they may be seen as debilitating falsehoods that block the development of human powers. The importance of an ethological reading of normativity becomes clearer at this point. A particular fiction is not 'good' or 'bad' in itself. Everything depends upon the total context in which that fiction operates – its 'goodness' or 'badness' will be relative to whether it increases or diminishes human understanding or flourishing.

Spinoza's treatment of 'essence' and right, God and Nature, laws and norms, is perplexing to Blijenbergh. He wishes to know if God as creator of all may be held responsible for the vicious acts committed by human beings; whether God will punish the wicked; and whether the knave and the honourable person are equally perfect in God's judgement. Spinoza (unsuccessfully) attempts to convince Blijenbergh that his questions are not well formed because they are based on a confusion of natural (or divine) laws and human norms. It is only human norms that involve judgement, and punishment for wrong-doing and reward for obedience. If the knave acts unwisely, ignorantly or without virtue, this is because he acts without understanding what he is, his context of action and the sources of the power he possesses. From the point of view of natural law, he is without virtue because he re-acts to his passions, and is therefore lacking in power. From the point of view of human law, he acts wrongly because he breaks the laws which serve to bind several bodies into one. The knave has the natural right to do all that he desires but this is not to say that his actions will bring him joy, or that his power is comparable to that of an honourable person. In placing himself outside the norms of the human community he acts in ignorance of his own nature and of the nature of the body from which he takes his life and derives his well-being. In Spinoza's terms, therefore, the knave cannot be seen to 'enjoy a better or more perfect life'.

In order to fully comprehend Spinoza's response to Blijenbergh, and the importance of virtue to collective endeavour, a deeper understanding of Spinoza's notion of virtue is required. In Part IV of the *Ethics*, Proposition 24, Spinoza writes: '[a]cting absolutely from virtue is nothing else in us but acting, living, and preserving our being (these three signify the same thing) by the guidance of reason, from the foundation of seeking one's own advantage'. Human individuals are not able to exist in isolation – this is determined by our place in nature 'wherein man is but a speck' (TTP: 202). We cannot not choose to live in communities of some kind since alone, 'no one would have either the skill or the time to provide for his own sustenance and preservation' (TTP: 73). Human life, *qua* human, is necessarily collective life, and collectivities can endure only if they are based on laws which promote, however imperfectly, collective human advantage. The natural right of each, when considered in isolation, 'is a nonentity, existing in opinion rather than fact, as there is no assurance of making it good' (TP: 296). It is only if, and when, these rights receive political sanction, in actually existing polities, that they become effective and carry normative force. It is to the advantage of each individual to respect these human laws because they have become the actual basis from which the natural right of each gains its collective, or political legitimation.

Certainly, there are better, and worse, foundations for societies, but any society which is to survive must minimally provide the necessities of life for its members. Benign rulers, just states, or tyrants are all bound by this requirement of governing. The norms which each type of sociability develops will be matched by a way of life that is more, or less, perfect, more, or less, virtuous. The virtue, power or right of each type of sociability cannot be determined by comparison with an abstract set of human laws, or with a moral doctrine based on mere human preferences. Rather, the virtue of each will be known by the form of life which each maintains, and the forms of human flourishing each endeavours to promote. No matter how powerful a particular regime is, it can never violate the laws of nature. As Spinoza wryly observed, authority is limited 'not only by the power of the agent, but by the capacity of the object. If, for instance, I say that I can rightfully do what I will with this table, I do not certainly mean, that I have the right to make it eat grass' (TP: 310). This limitation – imposed by the capacity of the object of command – serves to create various 'checks and balances' on the authority exercised by governments. Commands and decrees cannot alter the natural law which governs all finite modes and which necessitates that each strives to persevere in existence and to increase its powers of action. Tyrannies may well attempt to repress this drive or *conatus* but they cannot ever cancel it because it is an eternal natural law. To echo Foucault's well-known phrase: where there is power there will always be resistance. According to Spinoza, the governing body cannot rob people of their power of judging, or make them 'regard with honour things which excite ridicule or disgust' (TP: 310). Nor can it systematically flout its own laws, or engage in corruption, without ceasing to be a commonwealth. On Spinoza's view, to engage in such activities is to fail to be, or to cease to be, a government. A body that holds power in this fashion stands in relation to those it commands as a more powerful body stands to a less powerful body in the state of nature. It provides neither peace and security, nor the required conditions for human development. Individuals living under such a power are not bound by the social contract if that contract no longer has utility for them. Under conditions such as these, governing powers are as much at risk from their own subjects or citizens as they are from hostile external powers. Peace, as Spinoza says, 'consists not in mere absence of war, but in a union or agreement of minds' (TP: 317).

It is by considering the knowledge possessed by those who command that Spinoza distinguishes good governments from bad ones. There is no divine, or natural, power which will punish bad, or tyrannical, rulers for the oppressive or exploitative treatment of their members. Rather, there is the fact that such governments will not, and on Spinoza's view cannot, endure. Governments may be guilty of wrong-doing, or injustice, only in the sense that their acts deplete rather than enhance their own powers of governing because they fail to attend to the laws of nature. Such acts, according to Spinoza, are unreasonable and hence show a lack of virtue or power. The actual content of acts of governing which may be termed vicious (in this special sense of being unreasonable) cannot be known abstractly since it would depend upon the character of the ruling body, the characteristics of the governed body and the broader context in which the relation between the governors and the governed exists. Governments may have the right to coerce their members to behave as if they were rational but they cannot ever have the right to coerce rational members to believe irrational things. The latter kind of government, on Spinoza's view, ceases to be a government and becomes a mere collection of bodies engaged in combat with another collection of bodies – a state that is indistinguishable from civil war.

There are then resources in Spinoza's philosophy for distinguishing between legitimate, or virtuous, and illegitimate, or vicious, forms of authority. To say, as Spinoza undoubtedly does, that a body has the right to do everything that is within its power, is to say little more than that the laws of nature do not prevent actions and events that human beings find abhorrent and blameworthy. It is important to recall here that human beings do not comprise a 'dominion within a dominion' and what is consistent with natural law may be inconsistent with moral norms. This does not mean, however, that we are incapable of making normative or comparative judgements. Even within the range of legitimate polities, comparative judgements may be made. Spinoza distinguishes between governing by right and governing in the best possible way.

> It is one thing to till a field by right, and another to till it in the best way. One thing, I say, to defend or preserve one's self, and to pass judgement by right, and another to defend or preserve one's self in the best way, and to pass the best judgement; and, consequently, it is one thing to have dominion and care of affairs of state by right, and another to exercise dominion and direct affairs of state in the best way.
>
> (TP: 313)

The first aim of human society is to preserve its members by providing appropriate conditions for the pursuit of the necessities of life. These conditions include the provision of 'peace and security of life'. However, just as there is a difference between merely 'escaping death' and 'making use of life', so polities that promote the development of the capacities and powers of human being are more virtuous, and more powerful, than those that merely sustain life. Hence, those polities are best which do more than support human life, defined 'by mere circulation of the blood, and other qualities common to all animals'. The best polities are those which create harmonious conditions for the enjoyment of a fully human life, understood as a life defined 'above all by reason, the true excellence and life of the mind' (TP: 314). Again, the notion of harmony (agreement, union or concord) proves crucial to judging the best, most powerful and virtuous, collective body. Virtuous polities are those which combine the powers of many harmoniously and so constitute a body politic capable of functioning as if it were 'one mind and one body' (EIVP18S). What it might mean to speak of the polity as a unity will be considered in the following chapter along with the question of whether Spinozistic philosophy is capable of providing resources for contemporary democratic politics.

5   Freedom, authority and difference

On the last few pages of the unfinished *Tractatus Politicus*, Spinoza briefly alludes to the political significance of difference in democratic polities. He writes that democratic polities should exclude from active political participation all those who owe allegiance to other countries as well as those who cannot be classed as 'independent' and 'respectable'. The list of those excluded includes women, foreigners, slaves, children and criminals. The 'dependence' of women on men, of foreigners on other dominions, of slaves on their masters and of children on parents, disqualifies each group from the right to hold public office or to vote. This list of exclusions is not unusual in seventeenth-century political treatises. What is unusual is that Spinoza pauses to question the authority that men have over women – is this authority based in nature or convention? After a short and uncharacteristically poorly argued response, Spinoza ventures that women by nature have less power, and so less right than men.[1] At the very point where Spinoza considers the significance of conventional versus natural authority, the treatise abruptly breaks off with the words: 'But of this enough.' (TP: 387).

But it is not enough – even, or perhaps especially, for those who dwell in the present. Rather, the political implications of sexual, cultural and racial differences have become *the* issues of which we seem never to have had 'enough'. Many relations of domination and subordination that in the past drew their authority from nature are no longer sanctioned by democratic polities. The abolition of slavery and the women's suffrage movement have radically altered the face of democracy in the West. Contemporary feminist and 'post-colonial' political theory continue to challenge long-held distinctions between nature and convention. The expansion of democratic rights has not, however, led to the eradication of difference in the political realm. Rather, as one contemporary theorist has put it:

The global trend toward democratization is real, but so also are the oppositions and antagonisms asserting themselves against this trend in the name of various forms of 'difference' – ethnic, national, linguistic, religious, and cultural. Throughout the globe a new politics for the recognition of collective identity forms is resurging [and] identity politics is always and necessarily a politics of the creation of difference.

(Benhabib 1996: 3)

At the turn of the present century, the problem of difference continues to haunt democratic political theory and practice. The *prima facie* right to equal treatment and entitlements, perhaps ironically, has given rise to robust demands for the recognition of difference.

In the above passage Seyla Benhabib rightly points out that democratisation is 'global'. The phenomenon of 'globalisation' is not limited to capital, labour and information, but also includes the globalisation of human rights movements, multinational women's groups, a global multiculturalism, and transnational indigenous movements. This has led to a proliferation of multiple political identities each of which makes its own demands for social and political recognition. The political identities of individuals and of collective movements are no longer tightly bounded by, or limited to, sovereign states or geographical boundaries. These global movements also have generated imaginary communities whose extension is world-wide.

Obviously, this is a world of which Spinoza could not have dreamed. What then do we hope to achieve by the critical deployment of elements of his philosophical outlook in the present? Is Spinoza's political philosophy, as some have suggested (James 1996; Smith 1997), incapable of dealing with difference? This chapter is not only concerned to offer an interpretation of Spinoza's political theory, it aims also to bring Spinozistic insights to bear on our socio-political present. The readings offered in previous chapters of the materiality and sociability of the imagination, the 'transindividuality' which underlies processes of individualisation, and the historicity of norms, will be used to reflect upon contemporary social and political theory and practice. This chapter thus endeavours to think with, and beyond, Spinoza.

Freedom and authority in democratic polities

It may be difficult to see how Spinozistic politics – based as it is in 'power equals right' – has anything to offer the contemporary democratic spirit. Political authority, it would seem, is too readily reduced to holding the power to enforce arbitrary commands, and political freedom too easily to the capacity of an 'elite' to seize, maintain and enjoy such powers. On this view, authority and freedom, at least for the multitude, would seem to be oppositional terms. Further, as some have argued (Curley 1996), Spinoza's philosophy of immanent values and norms seems incapable of providing grounds by which one may judge one polity vicious and another virtuous. If these views were correct, it would be difficult to disagree with those who hold that Spinozistic political theory is impotent in the face of obnoxious forms of government and arbitrary power.

As we have seen, it is true that by Spinoza's lights those who have the power to dominate also have the right to dominate. It is also true that he held a conservative view of the capacities of the 'multitude' or the 'masses' (*vulgus*), observing that those who believe that the multitude may 'ever be induced to live according to the bare dictate of reason, must be dreaming of the poetic golden age, or of a stage-play' (TP: 289). However, because we are all subject to passions – especially those of fear and hope – '[a]ll are able to obey' (TTP: 199). This much is constant across types of individual and the times and places in which they dwell. It is from these unlikely premises that Spinoza builds not just a realist theory of the politics of domination but also a theory of political freedom and virtue. The ultimate 'task and the toil' of politics, for him, is not domination but enablement. Wise government does not seek to change those it governs into 'beasts or puppets' but aims rather 'to enable them to develop their minds and bodies in security, and to employ their reason unshackled'. In fact, he surmises, 'the true aim of government is liberty' (TTP: 259). Put differently, it is only through democratic structures of authority that true freedom may be realised.

In the last chapter we suggested that Spinoza's account of human being reveals both a passionate, or 'lupine' and a rational, or 'divine' order. Many commentators have tended to highlight one of these orders at the expense of the other which, unfortunately, results in an underestimation of the complexity and dynamism of Spinoza's views. A reading that does justice to the complexity of Spinoza's account of sociability and politics needs to acknowledge the manner in which each order implies the other. Perhaps the interpretive difficulty may be traced to the problem of how to assess the force of the determinism which runs through all of Spinoza's philosophy. How can one judge this behaviour lupine, or that behaviour divine, if every action is determined by causal forces rather than by free will or design? Spinoza's own response to this problem is that freedom, or liberty 'does not take away the necessity of acting, but supposes it' (TP: 296).

Freedom – individual and political – presupposes an understanding of the ways in which, individually and collectively, we are determined to act. The 'art' of wise government is thus twofold. First, institutions should be framed such that 'every man, *whatever his disposition*, may prefer public right to private advantage' (TTP: 217, emphasis added). Authority should be exercised in a way that guarantees the desired outcome but does not prejudge the reasons for action which bring about that outcome. Wise polities, that is, do not mystify the purposes, or the utility for all, of law and other institutions. Second, wise polities are ones which endeavour to maximise the rational powers of the multitude through education (EVP39S) rather than relying solely on eliciting compliance through appeal to the passions of fear and hope. Spinoza's determinism does not cancel the possibility of individual or political freedom. Rather, it functions to guarantee the success of wisely designed social and political institutions to act as 'second nature' determinants of human behaviour. The success of such institutions is to be measured by the degree to which they promote freedom in the citizenry.

Chapter 2 explained how, according to Spinoza, the freedom of individuals is expressed through their ability to understand the causes through which they are determined to act and through such understanding, to become the cause of their own actions. Such understanding involves critical reflection upon the imagination and affects which, in turn, may lead to their internal restructuring. Understanding the causes through which we are determined transforms passivity into activity, reaction into action. May an analogous claim be made with regard to Spinoza's political writings? Can we reflect upon and change the institutional determinants – the constitution, the laws, the social and political fictions – which structure collective life? In Chapter 5 of the *Tractatus Politicus* Spinoza considers why it is that the degree of peace and security individuals enjoy will vary according to the form of the state in which they dwell. His response is unambiguous: 'it is certain that seditions, wars, and contempt or breach of the laws are not so much to be imputed to the wickedness of the subjects, as to the bad state of a dominion'. He adds:

> if wickedness more prevails, and more offences are committed in one commonwealth than in another, it is certain that the former has not enough pursued the end of unity, nor framed its laws with

sufficient forethought; and that, therefore, it has failed in making quite good its right as a commonwealth.

(TP: 313–14)

The right of a commonwealth derives from its power and a commonwealth that has failed to frame its laws wisely lacks power. As such, it not only fails to restrain its citizens or subjects by law, it thereby fails also to provide the means through which its citizens or subjects may flourish. The two orders of human interaction – the lupine and the divine – are thus largely determined by better and worse political configurations of the very same natural forces and powers. The 'art' of wise government is to structure the field of human interaction in ways which minimise fear and suspicion whilst maximising the trust and confidence necessary for the flourishing of mutual aid and civic friendship (EIVP36S2). This is to construct a 'second nature' for human life but this 'second nature' is, and must be, consonant with the rest of nature. For Spinoza the second nature expressed through collective life is as necessary for the survival of human beings as water is for the survival of fish.[2] It is interaction with our fellow beings that defines our lives because a human life consists of more than the 'mere circulation of the blood, and other qualities common to all animals' (TP: 314). A truly human life consists of human flourishing and the development of human powers, especially the power of reason. The flourishing of individual understanding and freedom, in turn, assumes a 'transindividual' context of free relations and congenially bound affects. It assumes, that is, the structured organisation of power by wise institutions.

Human power, and the second nature to which it gives rise, is not of a different order to the power of nature. Nothing in nature prohibits political power from taking the form of domination or oppression. Such forms are, however, inconsistent with reason, which attends to specifically human interests. Non-democratic forms of polity divide human powers and so necessarily create less powerful collectives than those forms of government which endeavour to harmonise the power of all in order to realise and maximise human freedom. Powers that are in harmony, that is, powers that agree, are more powerful than comparable composites of power which are internally divided against one another. As the following passage makes clear, the transformation of natural right into political right – without loss to the individual – depends upon peaceful alliance rather than domination.

If two come together and unite their strength, they have jointly more power, and consequently more right over nature than both of them separately, and the more there are that have so joined in alliance, the more right they all collectively will possess.

(TP: 296)

What prevents individuals from combining their powers harmoniously is their passions. Spinoza was concerned to study the best means of minimising the harmful effects of human passions which so easily fluctuate between hope and fear, between love and hatred. The instability of the affects make human interaction unpredictable in detail but predictable in the misery that the fluctuations of the affects cause. The greater the degree to which laws and institutions are framed according to reason then the greater will be the degree to which the affects will be organised into stable and relatively congenial forms of sociability. This will always be a matter of degree, however, because no human collective will be without passion or disagreement.

The pertinent political opposition, for Spinoza, is not between authority, or power, on the one hand and freedom on the other, but between authorities that govern wisely and so increase the powers and freedoms of those whom they govern, and those that govern badly. 'A man who is guided by reason is more free in a state, where he lives according to a common decision, than in solitude, where he obeys only himself' (EIVP73). Membership in almost *any* polity is better than being stateless. However, within the range of types of polity, democratic polities are superior forms of organised authority because insofar as they promote the freedom of each, they increase the power of all and this 'power of all' is coextensive with the power of the polity.

We express human power or virtue when we act rather than when we are acted upon. 'But', as Spinoza writes, 'we act only insofar as we understand', so '[a]cting absolutely from virtue is nothing else but acting, living, and preserving our being (these three signify the same thing) by the guidance of reason' (EIVP24). This view is held consistently across Spinoza's metaphysical, ethical and political writings. It is understanding that represents our highest power, pleasure and virtue, and polities which promote these powers and pleasures are the best polities. Tyrannical polities may possess right but they do not thereby become rational. As Balibar explains, 'reason cannot be separated from knowledge, which is its intrinsic power. Therefore reason is useful, but not instrumental. It cannot be rational without also being reasonable' (Balibar 1997: 28).

Many forms of polity will exist because many have the power and therefore the right to exist. However, it is democratic polities that express the most powerful form of polity. But why should this be so?

Because democratic forms of polity enforce obedience to fundamental rules of law and other political structures *without removing the possibility of the development of reason*, which includes rational reflection on the utility of these institutions. The outward compliance with laws that are designed to maximise the rights which each has by nature, leaves open the motivation for such compliance. Certainly, compliance may signal fear of punishment but may equally signal an understanding of the purpose, design and benefit of such laws. In the first case, one obeys through the passion of fear, in the latter, through knowledge or virtue. The former person behaves like a slave, even if she or he lives in a democracy.

The best authority structures then are ones which are realistic about the need to regulate human passions without cancelling the capacity for all to develop reason. Acting virtuously, for Spinoza, always means acting to preserve oneself on the basis of an understanding of one's causal context. It is only through such understanding that one may endeavour to be in harmony with that context. The notion of harmony, or agreement in power, proves crucial to judging the best, most powerful and virtuous collective body. Virtuous polities are those which combine the powers of many harmoniously and so constitute a body politic capable of functioning as if it were 'one mind and one body' (EIVP18S3). When Spinoza writes about the 'best' polity as one in which the collective body functions as if it were 'one mind and one body', or 'as a man in the state of nature' (TP: 337), how literally should this unity be understood? And further, does a Spinozistic understanding of a harmony of powers exclude difference? These questions will provide the focus for the following two sections, respectively.

Political fictions and the social imaginary

Lee Rice has argued that those who seek to extend Spinoza's 'onto-logico-physical model of individuation', as presented in the *Ethics*, to an understanding of his political theory, seriously misrepresent Spinoza (Rice 1990: 271). He takes issue with those interpretations that read 'holistic' or 'organic' tendencies into Spinoza's account of the body politic. Rice counters these interpretations with the claim that Spinoza's political philosophy is 'radically individualistic' (Rice 1990: 274). Against the 'literalist' readings which treat the body politic as an actual individual, Rice poses those readings which claim that when Spinoza writes of the polity as an individual, he is speaking 'metaphorically'.[3] Den Uyl (1983) and McShea (1969), whose work we will discuss briefly, fall into this latter camp. For them, the state cannot be an individual or a 'superindividual'. Both philosophers understand Spinoza as a precursor of liberal political theory with a strong investment in an atomistic notion of the individual. McShea sees the state as little more than a mechanism which enables the management and distribution of the power of individuals across the political body (McShea 1969: 141–2). Den Uyl considers Spinoza to be a 'methodological individualist', that is, 'one who seeks to explain social phenomena in terms of the activities and relationships among individual agents' (Den Uyl 1983: 67). This approach rejects the notion of constitutive collective power in favour of a view which sees political power to be no more than 'the effective organisation of individual powers' (Den Uyl 1983: 71).

We are not so much interested in the details of Rice's account as we are in the way that it tracks the contours of the debate between communitarian and liberal accounts of political society. This debate, as Philip Pettit has noted, has 'mesmerised' contemporary political thought (Pettit 1994: 186). He cautions against accepting the sharply drawn oppositions between atomism/holism, individual/collective, and mechanical/organic, and argues that this dichotomous way of conceiving contemporary political theory does not exhaust the relevant options. Pettit offers republican political theory as a third term which re-positions these dichotomies in a non-oppositional fashion. In the final section of this chapter, we will suggest that contemporary extrapolations from Spinoza's political writings also can provide resources to challenge the dominance of the communitarian/liberal debate.

As previous chapters have shown, Balibar has offered a reading of Spinoza's theory of individuation as a relational ontology that is opposed to both classical individualism and organicism. Balibar holds that the individual, and the collective life in which he or she necessarily participates, are inseparable. Through the creation of the concept of 'transindividuality', Balibar argues that Spinoza's account of the individual may be interpreted as an account which treats individuals as necessarily connected to, and in constant communication with, other individuals. Moreover, because the individual is not a given 'substance' or 'subject', the creation of any particular individual always assumes a prior 'adaptive reciprocity' with other individuals, that is, 'a reciprocity of interconnected or interdependent processes of individuation and individualisation'[4] (Balibar 1997: 9). Comparing Spinoza and Leibniz, he argues that both:

> discovered that it is impossible strictly speaking to have a strong notion of singularity without *at the same time* having a notion of

the interaction and interdependence of individuals. Right from the beginning, the leibnizian and spinozistic theories imply that singularities are interconnected, building up a 'network' or a 'system'. We may conclude that in these doctrines the real 'object of thought' are not so much, in reality, the classical *extrema* (the Whole and the Element, or the Part), but rather the *reciprocal* viewpoints of unity and multiplicity, and the *relative* character of such notions as 'whole' and 'parts'.

(Balibar 1997: 9–10, n.9)[5]

Negri's interpretation of Spinoza's political and ethical writings shares this insistence on the double movement of the collective power of the multitude to constitute, and be constituted by, the multiplicity of individuals. There is no individual *human* life that can be separated from collective life and political existence is the natural, inevitable condition of human existence. The state, Negri writes, is:

a natural determination, a second nature, constituted by the concurrent dynamics of individual passions and guided toward this end by the action of that other fundamental natural power: reason; thus, it evades pessimistic individualism, contractual dialecticism, and Hobbes's absolutist organicism.

(Negri 1991: 110)

Both Balibar and Negri interpret Spinoza's concepts of individuality and community as reciprocal viewpoints rather than as oppositional terms. Their interpretations refuse the polarisation encouraged by the communitarian/liberal debate. One may find passages in Spinoza which support radical individualism and other passages which support the priority of collective life. But why should one set of passages be favoured at the expense of the other? In contrast to McShea and Den Uyl, whose interpretations focus on the political writings, Balibar and Negri tend to understand each component of Spinoza's philosophy – ethics, metaphysics and politics – as integral to, and consistent with, each other component. This is perhaps why, for the latter two philosophers, the constructive and productive role of the imagination is central to their interpretations.

If we hold that Spinoza's theory of the *materiality* of the imagination is vital to an understanding of the passions, sociability and political life then the truth value of fictions and metaphors becomes a more complex issue than Rice's reading allows. Spinoza's views on ontology and epistemology, as we have signalled earlier, are not so easily kept apart. Different ways of grasping one's context entail specific ways of being in that context.[6] Imaginative constructions of who and what we are, are 'materialised' through the forms of embodiment to which those constructions give rise. The imagination may create fables, fictions or collective 'illusions', which have 'real' effects, that is, which serve to structure forms of identity, social meaning and value, but which considered in themselves, are neither true nor false.

As the TTP demonstrates with reference to Judaism, socially shared fictions play a constitutive role in binding a group of individuals together. However, from an historical perspective, an individual born into such a group is confronted with the reality of these fictions. Such fictions will become constitutive of her or his 'identity' long before she or he becomes capable of actively participating in the conscious maintenance of such fictions through rituals or other forms of remembrance or validation. Further, a considerable passage of time elapses in individuals' lives before they may become capable of critical reflection upon the meanings, values and norms which have formed them. The truth or falsity of the fictions which found Judaism does not directly bear on the capacity of those fictions to create and maintain a way of life which, in turn, produces certain sorts of identities. The epistemologically pertinent point is not so much the literal or metaphorical meaning of the unity of the collective or political body; what is epistemologically pertinent is how one responds to the necessarily imaginative character of social, theological and political body composites. Here it seems necessary to maintain a distinction between those statements, ideas or imaginings which are meaning-generating and those which are true or false. The reading offered here of the materiality of the imagination, and its role in creating group and individual identities, shows how identity may be understood as an imaginary construction without thereby rendering identity 'false' or illusory.[7]

The ability of a political body to function as a unity, its coherence, derives from the fact that it has the power to make laws and form and maintain institutions for the execution of such laws. The degree to which these laws have utility for all will determine the degree to which such a body agrees with reason. However, no polity functions from the legislative, executive or other powers that it possesses, alone. Polities also cohere because they offer meaning and value to the lives of those who dwell within them. The affective investment of citizens, or subjects, in the political body is equally important to its viability. A sense of loyalty to one's fellows, a sense of belonging, a knowledge of the past of one's community, as well as shared goals for the future, are all important aspects of what it means to be a member of a larger body. These affective investments appeal more to imagination than reason, and pertain more to sociability than to pursuing one's individual advantage.

There is a long tradition in political philosophy of treating the laws of a body politic as analogous to reason in the individual. If this analogy is pursued in the context of Spinoza's political philosophy, it must be remarked that no polity can exist which is built on reason alone. Every polity is 'mixed' for the simple reason that human beings, no matter how rational, will always and necessarily be prone to the influences of the passions and imagination. Every body politic will be a mixture of rational laws and institutions, on the one hand, and fictitious constructions of collective identity, on the other. Moreover, fictitious entities exist in law (as will be discussed in the next chapter), founding institutions possess colourful narratives of their genesis, and social fictions may be more or less open to rational reflection and restructuring. It is in keeping with the reading we offer of Spinoza's philosophy that we avoid drawing sharp lines around reason and imagination. A democratic polity should be capable of tolerating rational reflection on, and criticism of, its constitutive fictions, including its legal fictions.

In *Imagined Communities*, Benedict Anderson also cautions against mistaking imaginative creations and fictitious inventions for falsity. He argues that 'all communities larger than primordial villages of face-to-face contact (and perhaps even these) are imagined. Communities are to be distinguished, not by their falsity/genuineness, but by the style in which they are imagined' (Anderson 1991: 6). Anderson's investigation of nationalism is different to the project pursued here but there are points of mutual interest. He, like Spinoza, is keen to understand how it is that 'men may fight as bravely for slavery as for safety, and count it not shame but the highest honour to risk their blood and their lives for the vainglory of a tyrant' (TTP: 5). Anderson's account of the human needs which are satisfied by membership in a nation bear on the affective and imaginative features of belonging to a community. Spinoza maintains that the formation of a body politic is necessary if natural right is to be expressed through politically sanctioned norms. It is to the advantage of each, and in accordance with reason, to endeavour to form such alliances with others. However, as we have tried to show, the formation of human communities, whether they be nations or not, also answers to human affective needs.

Part III of the *Ethics* considers a cluster of affects which describe the sociable dimension of our desires (EIIIP27f). Human beings desire to be well-regarded, they model themselves on those whom they believe to be honourable, they desire to be loved by those whom they love and so on. The fundamental passions of joy and sadness are played out in the social sphere as a disposition to form sympathetic and antipathetic attitudes toward others. If compositions of individuals are to endure, they will endeavour as far as possible to minimise antipathy and maximise sympathy among its parts or members. Fictions concerning the origins, values and identity of the collective body are one of the means through which collective bodies endeavour to endure by affectively binding each individual to all the others.

Anderson holds that the task of modern nations was to find a way to link 'fraternity, power, and time meaningfully together' (Anderson 1991: 36). Any community which is to outlast its founding members is faced with this task of creating a past and a future through which its members can make sense of their lives and deaths, their triumphs and sacrifices, and so invest not just their own lives but those of their children in the preservation of that community. When a member of any group, community or nation enjoys a sense of belonging and mutual endeavour that sense is largely produced through the imagination. This is not to say that membership in communities is illusory, rather it is to acknowledge that the very existence of human associations relies on the *power* of the imagination to bind the affects, as well as on the power of reason.

The argument pursued here throws the TTP into a new light. If theocracies built on fear and hope are not completely different in kind to democracies founded on reason, then how is one to judge between the two types of association? It is not the mere presence or absence of affect or imagination that distinguishes the two cases. Rather, the difference between the two lies in the extent to which the social, theological and political 'fictions', and the institutional forms, which found each are open to rational scrutiny and revision. This resonates with Spinoza's criticisms of theocratic rulers and the parables which they promulgate. The subjects of theocracies are prevented from forming an adequate understanding of cause and effect because the fictions which underlie theocracies confuse causes and effects. The result, as the last chapter showed, is a 'savage and sad superstition' which encourages people to think that sadness is pious and pleasure suspect (EIVP45C2 and S). Virtue is then seen as a means to an end (rewards in the hereafter) rather than an end in itself. Such fictions do not promote knowledge of one's power and one's place in nature but rather command an obedience to the power of others. Such forms of sociability are not criticised simply because they appeal to the imagination.

They are criticised because they appeal to the imagination in a way which hinders the development of reason. The resultant 'illusions of the multitude' are illusions which function to prevent the enhancement of their powers.

There is every reason to treat the *Ethics* and Spinoza's political writings as companion volumes which tell a consistent story about human ethical and political endeavour. Both the ethical and the political writings view the attempt to completely banish passion from human life as futile. Both are concerned with providing a method for transforming human passivity into activity, insofar as that is possible. Neither the political nor the ethical writings condemn imagination *per se*. Rather, the imagination is seen to provide a possible aid to the achievement of rational aims. The political fictions and social imaginary through which human beings necessarily form their second nature may be rationally transformed, or restructured, but not transcended. Such fictions and imaginings are – at least in part – constitutive of the normative elements of human identities and without them human life would enjoy no values at all. This is not to say, however, that one should be complacent about the values and norms to which we are born and in which we participate. It is the very immanence and historicity of forms of identity and their accompanying norms that allow a critical and reflective practice of reason to engage them. Furthermore, it is the immanence and historicity of these norms that render responsibility for them an entirely *human* affair.

The identity/difference dilemma

If Rice were correct about what he calls the 'literalist' reading of the individuality of the state or polity then he would be justified in viewing it as one which risks the danger of 'communalism', that is, a position which may lead to the denial of the autonomy of the individual (Rice 1990: 274). This 'communalism' – present in some forms of contemporary communitarianism – may conceive of the 'harmony' of collective bodies in ways which necessarily repress or exclude difference. However, as we have tried to show, the literalist/metaphorical dualism may not be the most productive way of understanding Spinoza's theses on harmony, individuality and community. The reading we offer does not posit an essential antagonism between collectively embodied powers and the powers of the individual. Indeed, we have suggested that Balibar's notion of transindividuality is a Spinozistic attempt to think unity and multiplicity as reciprocal rather than opposed viewpoints. But perhaps this reading may be accused of evading the crucial point: our disagreements with each other derive from our passions whereas agreement derives from reason, which is 'the same in all'. As some have argued then, the more wise a polity becomes, the more it will tend toward the promotion of sameness and the exclusion of difference.

Susan James, for example, has argued that Spinoza's conception of liberty is 'related to the exclusion of difference' (James 1996: 209) because the pursuit of freedom in the political realm consists in 'the overcoming of certain kinds of difference between individuals and in a shared aspiration to a degree of uniformity' (James 1996: 223). The wise polity, on her reading, is one governed by a 'good sovereign', that is, a sovereign who encourages citizens 'to act as they would if they were free, as they would if they were more alike than they in fact are' (James 1996: 208). There is much to commend in this reading of Spinoza's political views, and insofar as he is cautious about the capacities of the multitude to become reasonable, it accurately reflects one strand of his thought. However, the richness and complexity of Spinoza's thought, particularly the implications of his views on imagination and sociability, permit the development of alternative strands.

We have argued that democratic forms of polity are preferable to others because they encourage the development of the capacities of the minds and bodies of their citizens. We have argued further that ways of knowing oneself and one's context are reflected in embodied ways of being. What we know, imagine and believe is constitutive of our identities and these identities are processual, rather than fixed, because they are formed and re-formed through our participation in larger transindividual wholes. Reason itself, on this reading, is an immanent achievement of human collective endeavour, not an innate 'faculty'. The achievement of an agreement in power, or harmony of powers, is a state of affairs achieved in actual, historical time by embodied, actually existing, individuals.

The account of common notions offered in the last chapter showed the degree to which the development of reason, and the creation of the reasonable citizen, depends on our exchanges with others, and on our ability to become something other than what we were, through the collective endeavour to understand something we did not understand before. Encounters such as these are better understood as collective *transformations* of previous identities rather than the exclusion or overcoming of difference. The crucial respect in which this reading may be distinguished from others, is that we stress that the task of reason in the pursuit of liberty is the collective construction, in time, of something new, not the discovery of something which already existed.

In this sense, reason is an embodied capacity of an actually existing human collective which is endeavouring to preserve itself. This rational endeavour is virtue itself, according to Spinoza. As such, this virtuous endeavour transforms existing identities and differences into actively affirmed ways of life. Would these new ways of life dissolve prior differences? Hopefully, they would endeavour to transform those differences that draw their strength from oppressive power relations. Other differences, whose roots lie in shared memories, shared visions for the future, and shared conceptions of specific social goods, are bound to remain, albeit in revised forms.

Achieving a harmonious balance of powers within one polity does not imply the eradication of all differences. Indeed, the very notion of harmony assumes variation, not sameness. Moreover, citizens will never be without passions since they will always be acted upon as well as acting. Nor can any community survive without imagination, since every community exists in time and so will be faced with the necessity to construct, and reconstruct, an imaginary 'we' which founds and maintains any given form of sociability. The wise polity will not be one in which passion, imagination and difference are shed but rather one in which citizens will participate in the ongoing formation of the structures and institutions through which passion and difference are negotiated. Such participation will include critical reflection on, and transformation of, these institutions along with the social imaginary which supports them.

In Chapter 4 we argued that normativity, for Spinoza, is grounded in the judgements of political powers and institutions, including the historical legacy of past institutions that are continuous with those in the present. Right and wrong, justice and injustice, can only be conceived within organised communities (TTP: 208; TP: 298). Moreover, sin and merit are decided by common consent or sovereign decree (EIVP37S2). In contrast to natural law – which cannot be transgressed – normativity is a wholly human and fallible creation. Diversity in the normative commitments held by different groups, especially those held by different religious groups, is a prime cause of disagreement and disharmony. Remarking upon Spinoza's engagement with this problem in the TTP, Steven B. Smith writes that the Jewish Question 'remains the most vivid form of the question of the Other, or human diversity, with which liberal society has laboured to come to terms' (Smith 1997: xiv). He finds the treatment of this question in the TTP less than satisfactory and argues that Spinoza offered 'a strategy for dissolving group identities and differences not accommodating them' (Smith 1997: 201).

In the TTP, Spinoza's strategy to minimise the civil disharmony caused by diverse religious commitments was to offer seven dogmas of 'universal faith' as the foundation of a 'state religion', which would endeavour to represent the distillation of what is held in common by many religions (TTP: 186–7). Commitment to particular religions is not to be prohibited but rather is to be left to the privacy of individual conscience and faith. It is, perhaps, the fifth dogma that is central to Spinoza's attempt to create a universal religion that would unite rather than separate citizens: 'the worship of God consists only in justice and charity, or love towards one's neighbour' (TTP: 187). It is clear that Spinoza took Amsterdam as his model of a free society whose inhabitants held a liberal attitude towards difference and diversity:

> in this most flourishing state, and most splendid city, men of every nation and religion live together in the greatest harmony, and ask no questions before trusting their goods to a fellow-citizen, save whether he be rich or poor, and whether he generally acts honestly, or the reverse. His religion and sect is considered of no importance: for it has no effect before the judges in gaining or losing a cause, and there is no sect so despised that its followers, provided that they harm no one, pay every man his due, and live uprightly, are deprived of the protection of the magisterial authority.
>
> (TTP: 264)

The imposition of a minimum set of public norms to ensure a minimum standard of public behaviour does not cancel or exclude differences within the polity – not even religious differences. What it does endeavour to ensure – at least in democratic polities – is that no particular group may impose their normative commitments as *true for all*. As Spinoza makes clear, even the absolute sovereign, strictly speaking, has no right to claim that its laws are true because the force of juridical norms derives not from their truth value but solely from their utility and the ability of the sovereign to enforce them. If, as we have argued, democratic polities are distinguished by the degree to which they permit critical reflection on their institutions and laws then democratic polities are more able to acknowledge the immanence of normativity and to tolerate their peaceable transformation through time.

The historical transformation of the political status of women, slaves and others surely presents a case in point. The norms which once governed relations between men and women, slaves and masters, are no longer acceptable in democratic polities. This has radically changed the identities of, and differences between, women and men. The following chapter will make a similar point concerning the shifting norms which govern the relations between peoples who were colonised and their colonisers. Yet differences between men and women, and people from different cultures, still exist. In the present, it is these differences which demand political and cultural recognition. In the present we may think that the cases of sexual and racial differences are privileged because they are so clearly cases of *embodied* difference. However, the reading that we have offered of the materiality of the imagination, the transindividual nature of the formation of all identities, and the historicity of norms, implies that *all* difference is embodied difference. If some forms of identity seem 'neutral' or 'disembodied' then this reveals the extent to which the history of our norms continue to exert an influence on the ways in which self and other are able to be imagined.

Challenging one aspect of the imaginary which binds a particular collective, and which founds its institutions, inevitably upsets the coherence of the entire narrative. The effect of the expansion of democratisation, mentioned at the beginning of this chapter, has certainly transformed, at least partially, the ways through which we in the present experience being a woman or a man, being a descendent of colonisers or a descendent of those who were colonised. But the transformation has been partial only. The mere act of extending citizenship to individuals previously excluded will not automatically impart a sense of worth or belonging to those individuals. Politics is not simply a struggle over *ideas* and formal status. It also involves the struggle to embody and embed the desires, needs and imaginings of those whom democratic political structures in the present fail to adequately represent.

Anne Phillips has made a similar point with her distinction between a 'politics of presence' and a 'politics of ideas'. Phillips points out that liberal theorists have usually understood difference as amounting to diversity in opinions and beliefs. Previously excluded differences, understood in this way, may gain political representation by anyone who grasps the interests and beliefs of those who were excluded. As Phillips notes, 'when difference is considered in terms of intellectual diversity, it does not much matter who represents the range of ideas' (Phillips 1996: 141). Phillips questions the notion of a politics of ideas and argues that the assumption that one can separate ideas, beliefs and interests from the actual embodied presence of those who hold them, overlooks the complicated relation between ideas and experience. The embodied presence of previously excluded others prevents the liberal tendency to assume that ideas may be abstracted from the complex life experiences of those who hold them. She thinks that political structures may be developed which avoid an either/or choice between a politics of presence and a politics of ideas (Phillips 1996: 146–50). She also cautions that such structures must avoid understanding present differences in essentialist terms. That is, they must acknowledge that the processes of identity-formation and the negotiation of differences are fluid and open to revision. Phillips offers a potent account of why political presence matters but it is not clear from her analysis how individuals come to form the identities that they do, nor how identities may shift across time. The foregoing reading of Spinoza's views on individuality and community, reason, imagination and normativity may be helpful in articulating why a politics of ideas cannot be separated from a politics of presence.

The individual's endeavour to persevere will result in shifts in both its imaginings and its reasonings about itself and its context. These imaginings and reasonings in turn will cross from one individual to the next, from one group or community to the next. Individuals will compose new collectives and old collectives may be decomposed. In this way the hierarchical relations between groups always are open to restructuring. Political solutions will never be stable solutions and one consequence of understanding power as the very essence of the individual is that patterns of domination and subordination inevitably will meet with resistance from those whose power is thereby constrained. Those who benefit from relations of power which are structured by institutionalised relations of domination and subordination will, therefore, always be confronted with resistance to those relations. Any freedoms that those in the superordinate position enjoy will always be under threat from those whose subordinated conditions of life make such freedoms possible.

Those who now have been included within the body politic – who now enjoy the right to hold public office and to vote – nevertheless were excluded from participation in the historical shaping of the institutions, laws and norms, which now are assumed to be adequate to represent and protect us all. Such institutions, laws and norms are continuous with a past in which inequalities were sanctioned. This is of no little consequence to those in the present whose identities are continuous with groups that were subordinated in the past. Hence, their present identities may not enjoy appropriate levels of institutional recognition and the social imaginary may retain elements of their past status which continue to be damaging to them. The embodied presence of women, and other historically marginalised groups, in political, legal and other institutional arenas, is thus crucial if their changed formal status is to be practically recognised. Such recognition can not be reduced to mere cognitive change but must involve an affective and corporeal transformation of the way we experience self and other, identity and community.

Beyond the liberalism/communitarianism impasse

Spinoza has been claimed as the precursor of liberalism (Feuer 1964), libertarianism (Rice 1990), Marxism (Althusser 1997) and a 'holistic' communitarianism (Sacksteder 1975). Yet, as we have tried to show, Spinoza's philosophy evades comprehensive capture by any particular school of political thought. The reading of Spinoza's political philosophy that we offer refrains from claiming him for any particular camp. Rather, we have tried to show how his arrestingly fertile philosophy may provide resources for re-conceiving a range of issues in contemporary social, ethical and political life. We have suggested that a Spinozistic perspective may dissolve the false opposition between liberal and communitarian approaches by conceiving the distinction between individual and community in reciprocal rather than oppositional terms.

As Charles Taylor has pointed out, both liberalism[8] and communitarianism[9] are 'portmanteau' terms, each of which covers a broad spectrum of frequently incompatible views (Taylor 1995: 185). Nevertheless, a broad division may be drawn in relation to certain questions depending on whether one follows the liberal insistence on the priority of the freedom of the individual (the priority of the right) or the communitarian insistence on the logical and moral priority of the community (the priority of the good). Communitarians find liberals lacking insofar as they fail to acknowledge sufficiently the communal nature of identity formation and the socially embedded and embodied nature of the individual. Communitarians tend to stress the significance of community values and norms and the shared and public nature of social and political goods. In rejecting the individualism and universalism of liberal political philosophy, communitarians note that the individual is always constructed through social and political relations, specific institutions and culturally specific values.

However, the communitarian stance is not without its critics. Liberal political philosophers accuse communitarians of compromising the freedom of the individual, who risks being sacrificed to group interests, values and goals (Kymlicka 1990: 206–15). Feminists too have criticised communitarian philosophers for their conservatism, stating that they entertain 'a romantic and unrealistic vision of the past' and fail to provide conceptual tools for criticising present oppressive relations (Frazer and Lacey 1993: 130). What does communitarianism have to offer to contemporary political struggles – feminism, multiculturalism, indigenous politics – that strain against past values and practices? Frazer and Lacey capture the dilemma these groups may face if they reject the disembodied individual of liberal political thought. The risk, they write, is that we find ourselves:

> in the arms of the radically embodied communitarian self, a determined product of her or his circumstances, social conditioning and community culture. The situation of a being whose consciousness is determined by structure, communities, and institutions seems to be that of a helpless subscriber to the dominant conception of value. Arguably, the communitarian conception of personhood hardly deserves the name. At least in the context of a complex or pluralist society, it seems that the unity or even identity of the communitarian subject would break down as she is subsumed within a complexity of meaning-generating communities. If there is no self prior to or independent of its social constitution, it might be argued that the very idea of personhood becomes incoherent.
>
> (Frazer and Lacey 1993: 152)

The justifiable fear expressed here is that on some versions of the communitarian view, the self appears to completely dissolve into community along with any capacity to critically reflect on the social and political values through which individuals are formed. This view of the passivity of the self is part of the more general failing of communitarianism to articulate a theory of power. In fact, as Frazer and Lacey claim, a striking feature of the whole liberalism/communitarian debate is the omission of any adequate theorisation of power (Frazer and Lacey 1993: 31). We will return to this issue of power below.

From a Spinozistic perspective neither liberalism nor communitarianism *alone* is capable of accounting for the complicated relations between individuals and the communities in which they dwell. Aspects of both approaches are necessary in order to retain the rich complexity of human life expressed through a multiplicity of ethical, social and political relations. The problem with the liberal/communitarian debate is that it rigidly opposes worthwhile insights from each approach, when such insights should be combined. Charles Taylor has introduced a useful distinction between 'ontological issues' and 'advocacy issues' and argues that these two issues are continually confused in the debate between liberals and communitarians.

Ontological issues, he explains, 'concern what you recognise as the factors you will invoke to account for social life', or 'the terms you accept as ultimate in the order of explanation' (Taylor 1995: 181). At its extremes, the ontological issues decide who subscribes to the 'atomist' and who to the 'holist' schools of thought. Advocacy issues, on the other hand, 'concern the moral stand or policy one adopts' – individual rights versus the collective good. At its extremes, the advocacy issues decide who subscribes to the 'individualist' and who to the 'collectivist' schools of thought (Taylor 1995: 182). Taylor's point is that either position on the ontological issue may be combined with either position on the advocacy issue. In other words, one may be an ontological holist *and* an advocate of individual rights (Taylor 1995: 185). Taylor's four stances within the two issues represent the extreme cases at either end of each spectrum. Nevertheless, the distinction is important here because of the way it shows how the oppositional terms which underlie much contemporary political philosophy are open to challenge.

The reading that we have presented of Spinoza's democratic politics stands as an exemplar of an approach which sees the freedom of the individual and the authority of the community as, in principle, compatible. Spinoza's ontology and metaphysics contain holist aspects yet do not deny the force, the 'reality', or the 'right' of the individual. One may find both liberal and communitarian themes throughout Spinoza's writings, but these themes are not in tension with each other. At the level of ontological description, his writings present nature in holistic terms but this does not limit him to advocating a holistic, or communitarian, morality. On the contrary, we have seen that he does not confuse the descriptive and prescriptive elements of his thought. Human nature is determined by invariant natural laws *and* by the historically and culturally variable norms created by our 'second nature'. This second nature is causally connected to the same laws which govern the rest of nature, yet yield great variation across time and place.

Moreover, Spinoza's views on power are not vulnerable to the charge that Frazer and Lacey level at the liberal/communitarian debate, namely, that it lacks a theory of power. Power (*conatus* or virtue) is precisely what constitutes the individuality of the self and its strivings. What we are is determined by our pasts and the communities from which we draw our identities. These are the organised wholes through which our powers are enhanced or diminished, and through which the norms which govern our ethical lives are generated. However, what we will become depends, in part, on the vicissitudes of our *conatus*, the means through which we strive to understand who and what we are. For Spinoza, this is the extent of our freedom and it includes the individual and collective responsibility to play an actively critical role in what we will become.

Contrary to the view held by some communitarians, we do not simply 'discover' our (predetermined) identity, we also are determined to strive to understand, to maintain and, sometimes, to change it. The endeavour to understand and take responsibility for who we are was treated in Chapter 3. In subsequent chapters we considered the institutional and imaginary determinations of our norms, values and identities. How might this account of responsibility be deployed in a contemporary political context? The final chapter will explore this question with reference to Australia's 'post-colonial' present.

6 Responsibility and the past

In a letter to Hannah Arendt, Karl Jaspers paid tribute to Spinoza, describing him as 'this pure soul, this great realist, the first human being to become a citizen of the world'.[1] Spinoza's cosmopolitan sensibilities may be traced, in part, to his admiration for the Stoics who conceived of human beings as belonging to a universal 'cosmopolis' as well as to particular historical communities or states.[2] In Seneca's words, we should:

> take hold of the fact that there are two communities – the one, which is great and truly common, embracing gods and men, in which we look neither to this corner nor to that, but measure the boundaries of our state by the sun; the other, the one to which we have been assigned by the accident of our birth.[3]

Like the Stoics, Spinoza distinguished between 'individuals' and 'peoples', between membership in the general community of human beings and membership in particular communities. We become what we are through the collusion of two forces: (human) nature and what we have here called 'second nature'. Through the effects of this second nature, people may be distinguished 'by the difference of their language, their customs and their laws'. The effect of custom and law, in particular, is to create 'a peculiar disposition, a peculiar manner of life, and peculiar prejudices' (TTP: 232). This chapter will consider the present effects of past encounters between radically different peoples who did not share the same second nature but who, over time, nevertheless have become (formally) equal citizens in a shared polity. To what extent has the past identity of each been retained, and so to what extent do significant differences between the two groups remain? Finally, how do the different pasts of each affect the responsibilities they bear in the present?

Institutional inheritances and responsibility

The differences between one community, or state, and the next are created by the different ways in which each governs, conducts and imagines itself. The peculiar ways in which communities govern, conduct and imagine themselves, become entrenched in the institutions which serve to connect one generation of that community with its predecessors as well as with its successors, thus ensuring the continuity of identity. It is this very identity that will serve to differentiate one community from the next. In the absence of compacts, the relation of one state to another carries all the disadvantages of the relations between individuals in the state of nature (TP: 306).

However, polities no less than individuals, are determined to endeavour to accommodate themselves to others, to seek peace and the enhancement of their powers to survive, and to act rather than be acted upon. It is, then, in keeping with reason to endeavour to form amicable relations with other polities, wherever possible (TP: 306–8). It is only through such international compacts that freedom from the fear of external harm may be achieved. It is not difficult to suppose that Spinoza would look upon contemporary international alliances and transnational bodies, that seek to protect and enhance human well-being, with approval. The transindividuality that we have suggested characterises his theory of the emergence of individuality may be seen as relevant also to a contemporary global 'transnationalism' through which the identity of states, nations and other significant communities, are formed and re-formed. The circulation of images and affects through an increasingly international mass media present interesting possibilities – which will not be pursued here – for developing and extending Spinoza's views on the imagination, the contagiousness of the affects and the interconnectedness of all things. It is sufficient for our purposes to note the degree to which these new capacities for mass communication, across increasingly porous national and cultural borders, affect the formation of individual, cultural and national identities. These vastly expanded horizons of communication complicate the processes through which collectivities understand and account for themselves, as well as those through which they understand other collectivities and hold them accountable for their conduct.

The various demands for the recognition of difference that mark contemporary politics invariably include the demand to acknowledge the essential contestedness of stories and imaginings about the past of collective bodies, along with the enduring effects of those narratives in the present. The conflicted, and often bitter, disagreements that have characterised the Truth Commissions in Chile and Argentina, Bishop Tutu's Truth and Reconciliation Commission in South Africa, and the *Historikerstreit* in Germany,[4] attest to the political importance, for *present* identities, of *how*, and *by whom*, the past of a society is conceived, imagined and narrated. Which memories and narratives are endorsed by legal recognition, historians or the general public, matters to the ability of individuals and groups to imagine themselves as possessing a past, a present and a future, that is, as possessing an identity.

Memories that constitute the awareness of continuing existence through time are no less prerequisite for collective or national identity than they are for personal identity. Furthermore, as Charles S. Maier has argued:

> insofar as a collection of people wishes to claim existence as a society or nation, it must thereby accept existence as a community through time, hence must acknowledge that acts committed by earlier agents still bind or burden the contemporary community.
>
> (Maier 1997: 14)

Such claims return us to the issue of collective responsibility discussed in Chapter 3. What, following Tully, was there referred to as the 'strange multiplicity' of contemporary identities may be applied to the inner multiplicity of cultures, societies and nations, as well as to the inner multiplicity of contemporary selfhood. Part of the 'task and toil' of contemporary governments is to recognise and negotiate this internal cultural diversity, and their successes and failures are now judged on a global as well as a local stage.

Passions, such as shame, pride, guilt and anger, now circulate on an international scale and each society or nation takes an interest in the methods employed by other societies or nations to foster social harmony and to deal with internal disharmony. The greater the degree to which any given society or nation sees itself as similar to another, the greater the probability that it will measure its normative commitments and institutional structures against that other. This is certainly the case with contemporary democratic societies whose origins lie in the West. For example, a shared past in British and European traditions and institutions may be seen to provide enduring patterns of identification amongst the peoples and governments of North America, Canada and Australia. All are 'postcolonial' societies that today are defined by multicultural identities that include, however ambivalently, indigenous peoples.

The demand from indigenous groups for the recognition of their difference raises the issue of collective responsibility for the past in particularly stark terms. Contemporary liberal democracies that have developed from colonial societies present paradigm cases of the enduring presence of past encounters with radical difference. The starkness of such cases derives from several features. First, from the point of view of the colonised, the encounter was involuntary and violent. Second, the differences between the colonisers and the colonised in language, customs and laws – the second nature mentioned above – were so extreme that indigenous peoples often were not even recognised as possessing law, social institutions or sovereignty. Third, the failure to recognise cultural difference most often resulted in a failure to recognise the common humanity of those who were colonised and so frequently they were treated with less concern and dignity than animals. Finally, the exclusion of colonised people from active participation in the creation of the 'new' society, of course means that the institutions of contemporary democratic societies – which are continuous with those of the past – embody the very norms, interests, understandings and imaginings of those whom they were designed to serve. The corollary of this claim is that these same institutions oppress, marginalise or, at best, ignore those who did not figure in their design.

Any present indigenous challenge to the dominant ways of life, customs and prejudices of the colonisers must thus be made within the framework of those very institutions and laws through which the second nature of the colonising group was, and continues to be, expressed and validated. It is perhaps under conditions such as these that the historical and cultural specificity of norms, and the fictive dimensions of law, may account for the astonishing, but largely unacknowledged, power of the social imaginary of the dominant group.[5] Previous chapters have argued that the historical and immanent nature of normative commitments renders them a wholly human responsibility. In this chapter we seek to explore what this responsibility involves for those groups whose norms have become the institutionalised standard by which all are heard, measured and judged.

The socially responsible exercise of this largely inherited power should include the preparedness of those in the present to reflect upon, and change, those norms and laws that cause harm to present-day indigenous peoples. The responsibilities for the past, that contemporary dominant groups collectively bear, include their willingness genuinely to share the two public goods identified by Tully, and discussed in Chapter 3. First, those who enjoy the benefits of democratic society bear the responsibility to develop the capacity for 'critical freedom', which includes cultivating 'the ability to see one's own ways as strange and unfamiliar, to stray from and take up a critical attitude towards them and so open cultures to question, reinterpretation, negotiation, transformation and non-identity' (Tully 1995: 206). Second, those who dwell within democratic societies have a responsibility to acknowledge that all are entitled to 'the aspiration to belong to a culture and a place, and so be at home in the world' (Tully 1995: 202). The sharing of these two public goods necessarily involves seeing one's own social imaginary, the second nature which has become embedded in our social institutions, as one among many ways of being human. Put differently, ways of being a citizen of a specific polity should not overide the duties of being a 'citizen of the world'. As we will argue at the close of this chapter, it is a limitation of the colonial imaginary that it measures all ways of life in terms of its own conception of 'civilisation'. The following sections will consider a contemporary Australian example of an indigenous challenge to colonial law which lays bare the incompatibility of the imaginaries of the colonisers and the colonised. This example will be used to draw out how the Spinozistic perspective, developed in previous chapters, can provide alternative ways of understanding the operations of power, imagination and normativity in contemporary political life.

Conflicting imaginaries: *terra nullius* and *Mabo*

In 1992, the legal fiction that Australia was *terra nullius* prior to British colonisation was overturned by the High Court in the *Mabo* judgment.[6] Eddie Mabo was one of five people who took a claim to the High Court of Australia for the legal recognition of their traditional ownership of land in the Torres Strait area, an area which had been annexed to the Australian state of Queensland in 1879. Mabo and others claimed that their entitlement to their land derived from their membership of an organised social group, governed by law, who had occupied and cultivated their land continuously since colonisation. Their claim was a direct challenge to all the assumptions underlying the 'settlement' of Australia. As Kamal Puri explains:

> *Terra nullius* is a well-established concept of the common law. The law in force in a newly-acquired territory depends on the manner of its acquisition by the Crown. There are three ways of acquiring

sovereignty over a new territory – by conquest, cession, or occupation. For the purposes of identifying the law of a new British
colony, the English common law has traditionally made a distinction between colonies where sovereignty was established by cession
or conquest and colonies where sovereignty was established by
settlement or 'occupancy'. In cases of cession and conquest, the
local laws of the relevant territory remained intact ... in the case
of a settled colony, the common law, as was reasonably applicable
to the circumstances of the new colony, was introduced.

(Puri 1993: 146–7)

Acquisition of territory by occupation assumed the doctrine of *terra
nullius*, whose extended legal meaning included not only uninhabited
land but also territories that were inhabited by peoples who did not
cultivate the land, who were not seen to form an organised society
governed by law and so who were deemed to be 'uncivilised savages'.

What Mabo and others succeeded in demonstrating to the High
Court was that the situation of their lands before and after colonisation was not *terra nullius*. Moreover, in what is seen as a contentious
decision (see Moens 1993), the High Court commented that its judgement in the case of *Mabo* had implications for the relation of all
indigenous Australians to land, not just for the traditional owners in
the Torres Strait. In making this judgment, reference was made to the
necessity to bring Australian law in conformity with international law,
to the unacceptable racist assumptions which underlay the prior judgement of *terra nullius* and to the need to treat indigenous Australians
with the respect and dignity that their common humanity demands.
Hence, the legitimacy of contemporary Australians' relation to land;
their relation to their past, and hence to their future; and finally, their
relations with each other, were all radically unsettled by the *Mabo*
judgment.

The *Mabo* judgment has had far-reaching consequences for indigenous title to land; for the present legitimacy of traditional indigenous
law; and for the mining, pastoral and other economic interests of white
Australia. These questions, while important, are not the focus of our
concern here. Others have written knowledgeably on these questions,
which require considerable expertise in law, history and anthropology.[7]
Rather, we seek to explore the repercussions of the *Mabo* judgment on
the social imaginary of contemporary Australia and the manner in
which responsible reflection on, and transformation of, that imaginary
involves the exercise of an important freedom of citizenship. It
involves, in other words, the responsible exercise of the enjoyment of

the two public goods – the exercise of critical freedom and the acknowledgement of the right of all to a sense of belonging – described by Tully.

When Paul Keating, then Prime Minister of Australia, launched the 1993 International Year for the World's Indigenous People, the *Mabo* judgment was clearly uppermost in his mind. The speech he made to launch the Year stressed the centrality of the imagination to the identity of the Australian people. He spoke of the necessity for non-indigenous Australians:

> to recognise that they [indigenous Australians] are part of us, and that we cannot give indigenous Australians up without giving up many of our own most deeply held values, much of our identity – and our own humanity. ... the starting point might be to recognise that the problem starts with us non-Aboriginal Australians. It *begins*, I think, with that act of recognition. Recognition that it was we who did the dispossessing. We took the traditional lands and smashed the traditional way of life. We brought the diseases. The alcohol. We committed the murders. We took the children from their mothers. We practised discrimination and exclusion. ... we non-indigenous Australians should try to imagine the Aboriginal view.[8]

Keating's speech stressed the importance of exercising the imagination in the processes of recognising and negotiating differences which have the potential to divide, as well as to unite citizens. He also appealed to non-indigenous Australians – the 'we' in his speech – to accept responsibility not just for the present condition of indigenous Australians but also for the way in which the past actions committed by their colonising forebears continue to dwell in the present.

For many, it is incoherent to speak of the collective responsibility for actions committed by others, in a past with which the present is continuous. Many contemporary moral philosophers dismiss the idea of collective responsibility – in either a philosophical or a juridical sense – as the product of muddled thinking. Those who could not act in a past because they did not exist, cannot be held responsible for that past. On this interpretation, national or group identities cannot be seen as genuine because they compose only *imaginary* wholes. There are two broad bases on which this view is open to challenge. First, juridical systems provide institutionalised continuity for the norms which govern the relations between individuals who share, however unevenly, the benefits and burdens of dwelling within a single polity.

Hence, laws sustain a strong diachronic connection between those who dwelt in the past and those who dwell in the present, as well as a synchronic connection between those who dwell in the present. These connections confer various rights and duties on us, as will be discussed in the following section. Second, those who reject the idea of collective responsibility for the past fail to attend sufficiently to the force of the imagination in social and political life, a force which we have stressed throughout previous chapters. The importance of critically reflecting upon the imaginary through which we are formed will be the focus of the final section in this chapter.

Are 'we' responsible for the past?

The political and ethical problem presented by the account of the social imaginary developed in previous chapters is its *permanence*. As Spinoza remarks, those who assume that human beings may come to act from reason alone, do not produce political theory but merely satirical accounts of chimerical beings whom no-one has ever encountered (TP: 287). Spinoza's account of the imagination is not a theory about a 'faculty' but a theory about a permanent structure through which human beings are constituted as such. This structure, as we have seen, expresses a relational or transindividual ontology. The strength of the social imaginary is that it constructs a logic of its own – a logic which cannot be shaken or undermined simply by demonstrating the falsity of its claims, its inherent contradictions or its aporias. The social imaginary is constitutive of, not merely reflective of, the forms of sociability in which we live. The imaginary endures through time and so becomes increasingly embedded in all our institutions, our judicial systems, our national narratives, our founding fictions, our cultural traditions.

The feeling of belonging to this or that family, clan or nation, confers upon us both benefits and burdens or obligations. One of these obligations is to take responsibility in the present for the manner in which one's constitutive imaginary harms, excludes or silences others. It must be admitted that one hardly has to seek out such responsibilities. The ethical and political demand to take up one's responsibilities comes from those who continue to be harmed in the present. One of the social goods which is constitutive of our very identities is the habitation of an imaginary which enhances our powers of action by providing a ground for our feelings of belonging and our claims to social, political and ethical entitlements. Ethico-political life demands that we exercise judgement, make choices, select from possible futures, and invent new strategies for coping with change. The demand for change frequently issues from others whose imaginaries only partially, and perhaps involuntarily, overlap with our own.

Although imaginative and affective identification with others is one of the processes through which collective life is formed, it is not the only process. Previous chapters have described the power of collective bodies to select, create or invent, a milieu in which the powers of acting to preserve themselves may be enhanced. That is, past experiences may yield life-enhancing norms of action which become institutionalised in the present, especially through custom and law. Wise governments will legislate in ways which promote harmony among individuals. This is why Negri, while acknowledging the destructive and superstitious tendencies of the imagination, nevertheless highlights its potential liberatory force (Negri 1991: 86). In a similar vein, Deleuze sees in Spinoza's theory of the affects a pre-Nietzschean tendency to define reason as a particularly powerful type of affect that at its highest power seeks social harmony and mutual empowerment (Deleuze 1990: 255–72). These readings of Spinoza do not posit reason and affect in oppositional terms. A Spinozistic perspective on an institution, such as law, can reveal its affective and imaginative, as well as its rational components.

Gerald J. Postema has written about the moral presence of our past in a way that resonates with some of the points we have made concerning the materiality of the imagination and the historicity of norms. He writes that '[i]n law, as in much of the rest of our lives, the past is present in our moral or practical deliberations in the form of precedent' (Postema 1991: 1156). We make and keep promises, we enter and honour contracts, and we engage in collective action with others, always imagining that others will keep their promises, honour their contracts and contribute to collective endeavours. Postema argues that past decisions, actions and commitments not only give shape to the paths of action open to us in the present, they also mould the desires and values through which we will conceive and judge those options (Postema 1991: 1155). Remembering and honouring past experiences and commitments that we have shared as a community, will form the basis of the identity of our community. In law, as in the lives of individuals, keeping faith with preceding actions and norms is constitutive of the integrity of the practices which constitute identity.

Central to the identity of democratic polities is the idea that every citizen is entitled to be treated equally by their governing institutions. This defines an important part of what it is to enjoy membership of a democratic community. As Postema points out, the entitlement to equal treatment unites us both horizontally and vertically with other members of our community. Horizontally, by organising the normative relations between one member and the next; and vertically, by relating the institutions which embody the normative commitments of a community to each individual across time. The loyalty that we feel to the institutions which govern us derives, in large part, from the pride we take in their ability to act meaningfully and with integrity which, in turn, allows us to plan our lives accordingly. Laws, including precedent, function to give shape to the community in a manner analogous to the function of memory for the individual. Thus, Postema argues, 'we can trace the importance of the moral presence of our past, and of precedent in particular, to the duty to keep faith with each other, in both dimensions of our communal relations' (Postema 1991: 1176).

Postema's thesis is particularly interesting to consider alongside the *Mabo* judgment. The High Court was put in the unenviable position of judging between honouring the rights of contemporary indigenous Australians to be treated as fully fledged members of society, and so deserving of recognition, respect and dignity, on the one hand, and respecting the integrity of the judgments of law and precedent on the other. By Postema's standard, the High Court made the right judgment. There are conditions under which being loyal to the institutions that should serve all members of the community involves breaking with precedent and with past normative commitments. In a phrase which carries considerable resonance with Tully's notion of 'critical freedom', Postema argues that we should embrace a Nietzschean 'critical history'. Critical history, he writes:

> involves simultaneously an *interpretation* and an *indictment* of current and perhaps long-standing behaviour of members of a community, indictment made in terms of the commitments and ideals of that community. This view treats 'mistakes' not merely as theoretical anomalies, but as behaviour for which participants at the time, and those who inherit the practice, are accountable.
>
> (Postema 1991: 1179)

The founding fiction of colonial Australia – a fiction which for over 200 years enjoyed the force of law – was the 'discovery' of a vast, and at least for legal purposes, empty continent. Australia was imagined as a continent devoid of law and society, and so without a history. The fantasy of Australia as a *tabula rasa* could only be maintained by the attempt to literally erase its indigenous inhabitants, along with their laws, customs and systems of kinship. No-one alive today may be held responsible for acts that were committed in the eighteenth and nineteenth centuries – acts which included mass murders, the poisoning, rape and literal enslavement of Aborigines. What we are responsible for is the way in which the past endures in our present – both in the form of inherited practices and as memory. How we remember, commemorate or deplore the past matters to our present relations with different others. How we configure the past also matters to the way in which that past is converted into practices and values which will inform our future. The social imaginary in which, and through which, Australian nationhood and the categories of 'black' and 'white' have been formed, must be transformed.

The *Mabo* judgment disturbed not only mining, farming and other financial interests of present-day non-indigenous Australians, it also severely disturbed the social imaginary which grounds the 'we' of contemporary Australian identity. This imaginary is the site and cause of direct and indirect harms experienced by indigenous Australians. No amount of redistribution of goods, compensatory financial arrangements, or even the return of land will cancel or alleviate the past and present effects of the European imaginary on indigenous peoples. This is not an argument *against* redistribution, compensation, or the return of land. Rather, these measures, though necessary, are far from sufficient. It is here that the 'we' of Keating's speech is crucial. Who – if not 'we' – possesses the capacity to accept responsibility for the harmful effects on others of the social imaginaries which we inhabit and which have formed us as the types of persons we are? Responsibility for our social imaginary can only be a *collective* responsibility that 'we' take up *toward* the past. While there is no 'outside' of the social imaginary this does not mean that we are entirely determined by it. No social imaginary is sealed but rather consists of multiple and overlapping imaginaries. Encounters with significantly different others may open one imaginary to another, offering perspectives and opportunities for the re-negotiation of identity as well as occasion for conflict.

Recognition, freedom and history

The fundamental insight of liberatory movements is that freedom is not a possession of the autonomous individual but rather an ethico-political practice that may be actualised only in common with others. Genuine freedom always involves a collective process of *becoming*-free. This collective process of becoming-free is inseparable from the broader question of understanding how we have become what we are today. While it may be incoherent to claim that we are *blameworthy* for the type of community through which we have been formed, and which 'inhabits' us quite as much as we 'inhabit' it, becoming-free is a practice which will inevitably involve *taking on* responsibility for the manner in which we carry this imaginary into the future. Such responsibility, we argue, includes endeavouring to transform those aspects of our imaginary which are harmful to others. The social imaginary may be inescapable but it is not, for all that, fixed. Its reiteration and repetition through time opens possibilities for it to be (re)constituted differently. The collective transformation of the social imaginary cannot be 'thought' voluntaristically or relativistically as pure (re)invention of the past. Rather, it must be thought collectively, which is to say it must be thought and negotiated with actually existing different others in historical time.

To draw out the importance of the embodied and temporal dimensions of re-negotiating our differences we need to return to several points made in previous chapters. In Chapter 4 we argued that Spinoza's political philosophy offered a wholly immanent, or naturalistic, reading of sociability that posits the gradual or incremental development of our institutions. This reading of the emergence of social structures sees them as constituted through ongoing and open-ended practices to which each generation contributes through their acts and their imagination. Thus, membership in a democratic polity carries with it both freedoms and responsibilities: the freedom to contribute to the shape which contemporary institutions take and the responsibility to exercise this freedom in a way which respects others. The aim of democratic societies, on this reading, is to endeavour to achieve a harmony of powers among its members.

Spinoza's politics of power, we suggested, may profitably be understood in terms of an ethology – a theory of the capacities of bodies for affecting and being affected. This ethological approach emphasises three aspects of Spinoza's ethico-political theory. First, the materiality of the power of the affects yields particular, rather than universal notions of 'good' and 'bad'. Second, ethology shows how the powers of bodies are determined by the wider context in which they act and are acted upon, which includes the second nature of human being. And finally, ethology accounts for the formation of communities in terms of compositions based in agreement between bodies. This endeavour to harmonise human encounters is dependent on the development and maintenance of just institutions. Our preference for reading Spinoza's theory of power in terms of an ethology (rather than a morality) bears on the themes of this chapter. Ethology studies the *ethos* of bodies – in the broadest sense of that term – and so does not make moralistic judgements that inevitably measure difference in terms of superior and inferior ways of being. Rather, each way of being may be understood as a more, or less, successful experiment to create a sustainable 'world'.

The question raised by colonisation is what happens when two very different worlds collide? How, if at all, may they harmonise? In Chapter 5, we applied Anne Phillips' notion of the 'politics of presence' to a Spinozistic understanding of the political problem of difference, arguing that the embodied presence of marginalised groups is necessary if the norms, institutions and imaginary of a community are to be transformed. Those who have been marginalised by the communities in which they – voluntarily or involuntarily – dwell cannot be recognised *in their difference* unless the 'world', the *ethos* from which they draw their power to act, and their very identities, is recognised. Negotiating difference necessarily involves the embodied presence of the relevant parties because negotiating difference involves negotiating (at least two) 'worlds'. The past – of all parties – will inevitably figure in these negotiations because each is what she or he is in virtue of the way in which the past informs, forms and dwells in the present. Moreover, as the *Mabo* judgment has shown, the past can unexpectedly disrupt the linear time of history, re-opening the past to new interpretation.[9]

The collision of European and indigenous 'worlds' provides perhaps the starkest example of difference. The norms, laws and *ethos* that have their basis in European cultures cannot be understood independently of the past which has made those cultures what they are – in all their multiplicity – today. Likewise, the norms, laws and *ethos* that have their basis in indigenous cultures cannot be understood independently of the past which has made those cultures what they are – in all their multiplicity – today. The process of de-colonisation cannot avoid dealing with these multiplicitous pasts in the endeavour to negotiate a just and fair present for all. *Mabo* may have come as a shock to non-indigenous Australians, shaking their imaginary at its foundation. Presumably, *Mabo* had a very different effect on indigenous peoples, whose way of being is essentially tied to their relation to land. When Galarrwuy Yunupingu, an indigenous Australian, spoke to a summit about how indigenous and non-indigenous peoples in Australia may reconcile farming, mining and traditional interests in land, he made the point that indigenous law had still not been understood, never mind respected or accepted. He said that:

[a] simple white man's paper cannot extinguish a traditional law, the culture, the language, the painting on the rocks, the painting on the barks, the painting on the bodies. ... The Aboriginal Law still stands where it cannot be seen. It's in the river, it's in the bill-abong, it is in the rock, it is in the caves, it is in the sea, the law still remains. It remains intact as it was for the last 60,000 years or maybe more.

(Cape York Land Council 1997: 68–9)[10]

Of course, this statement could be understood as mere metaphor – as an instance of a 'primitive' cosmogony – but this would surely miss the point that to those whom it sought to erase, the doctrine of *terra nullius* was no more or less a fiction, part of an elaborate and alien imaginary.

Both non-indigenous and indigenous laws reflect the different ways of knowing and ways of being that characterise the two groups. Each has its second nature, its *ethos* and imaginary, which connects each to its past and allows it to imagine a future. If a shared future, based on harmonious relations, is to be achieved, then these differences will need to be negotiated in a way which acknowledges the specificity of each. Yunupingu suggests 'the proper way' of doing this: 'You come to my law, and my law will sort out your law, and your law sort out my law, and we sit down face to face and sort out where the best ground that you and I will talk and agree' (Cape York Land Council 1997: 69). The negotiation of two laws will involve what Tully has called 'critical freedom': the exercise of the capacity to see the specificity of one's own world as one among others. This, in turn, supposes that we are capable of reflecting on our present through Postema's notion of 'crit-ical history'. Along with the Stoics, this would be to conceive of one's own form of sociability as a valued but contingent way of life that does not cancel one's responsibilities as a 'citizen of the world'. On this view, 'world citizenship' does not involve an 'idealistic', or unattain-able, transcendence of embodied being, but rather an immanent, embodied and ongoing negotiation between multiple forms of socia-bility.

Notes

Introduction

1 For example, Yirmiyahu Yovel has drawn attention to Spinoza's legacy of Marrano traditions in which it was an accepted practice to conceal intended meaning behind the mask of conventional language (Yovel 1989a: 29). Steven B. Smith makes a similar point in his recent study of Spinoza, reminding us of Spinoza's notoriety 'for using traditional religious language and imagery to mask his new, fundamentally irreligious teachings' (Smith 1997: 142). Finally, Douglas Den Uyl also acknowledges Spinoza's subversive usage of standard terms in seventeenth-century philosophy (Den Uyl 1983: 106).

2 Comprehensive and integrated treatments of Spinoza's ethical, political and metaphysical thought are uncommon in the Anglo-American philosophical traditions. 'Continental' philosophical traditions more commonly treat Spinoza's *Ethics* and political writings together. For a recently translated example of this approach, see Balibar (1998).

1 Spinoza's imagination

1 Lucretius (1975: 113) Book 2, lines 216–25.
2 Lucretius (1975: 203–5) Book 3, lines 177–207.
3 Lucretius (1975: 279) Book 4, lines 26–44.
4 Lucretius (1975: 281–2) Book 4, lines 54–90.
5 For a helpful discussion of Stoic notions of body and of the 'incorporeals' see the commentary provided by Long and Sedley (1987: 164–6).
6 Letter 17, 20 July 1664, in Curley (1985: 352–4).
7 The intricacies of this 'logic' of the interactions of imagination and affects are elaborated in Michèle Bertrand's excellent discussion (Bertrand 1983: 78–90).
8 In calling attention to the ways in which the passions can be transformed through critical reflection on the images and fictions around which they are organised, Spinoza echoes Hellenistic sources, although those sources emphasised the role of belief rather than imagination in structuring the emotions. Martha Nussbaum has shown, in an interesting discussion of the treatment of sexual desire in some of these ancient sources, that Aristotle, the Stoics and Epicureans had all seen desire as structured by

beliefs, and hence as contingent and changeable – both indirectly through cultural change and more explicitly through a 'therapeutic' resort to philosophical reflection, shedding 'cultural fantasies' to form 'new habits of attention, new patterns of desire'. Nietzsche, as Nussbaum points out, was profoundly influenced by Hellenistic philosophy; and is closely allied with Stoicism and Epicureanism in his commitment to an ideal of radical criticism of convention – to the idea that there is 'a healthy element in the human being that can flourish if, and only if, certain deep cultural conventions are criticised'. The Hellenistic tradition of writing about emotion and desire, Nussbaum argues, sees philosophical education and argument as 'the instruments of freedom for the individual, and, for the community, the bases of universal citizenship in a truly rational society' (Nussbaum 1996: 195–216). I discuss the educational implications of Spinoza's critique of fictions in Lloyd (1998).

9 Spinoza, *Treatise on the Emendation of the Intellect*, in Curley (1985: 27), Section 58.
10 Letter to Schuller for Tschirnhaus, in Curley (1994: 268).
11 In the use of the term which is relevant here the connotations of the 'imaginary' are not the 'unreal' as distinct from the real 'perceived'. When modern social theorists talk of an 'imaginary' they mean, rather, a loosely connected set of images embedded in social practices, or throughout literary or philosophical texts. The term 'imaginary' is used in this extended way in, for example, the translated title of Michèle le Doeuff's study of philosophical imagery, *The Philosophical Imaginary* (1989). It occurs also, in a different but related sense derived from the work of Jacques Lacan, in the work of Luce Irigaray (1985); and as the 'social imaginary' it is a central concept in the work of Cornelius Castoriadis (1994).

2 Spinoza's freedom

1 For an informative treatment of the contrasts between Stoic versions of freedom and ideals of free will which derive from biblical sources, see Dihle (1982).
2 Fragment from Gellius, in Long and Sedley (1987: 388).
3 Fragment from Alexander, 'On Fate', in Long and Sedley (1987: 390).
4 Fragment from Gellius, in Long and Sedley (1987: 388).
5 Fragment from Diogenianus, in Long and Sedley (1987: 389).
6 For an elaboration of this identification, see the editors' commentary on Stoic approaches to moral responsibility in Long and Sedley (1987: 394).
7 Fragment from Cicero, 'On Fate', in Long and Sedley (1987: 388).
8 Fragment from Epictetus, *Discourses* 1.1.7–12, in Long and Sedley (1987: 391).
9 Tschirnhaus, Letter to Spinoza, 8 October 1674 (Letter 57), in Curley (1994: 267).
10 Spinoza discusses the same examples at EIIIP2S.
11 Letter to Tschirnhaus (Letter 58), in Curley (1994: 267).

3 Re-imagining responsibility

1 Fragment from Gellius, in Long and Sedley (1987: 336).
2 Fragment from Stobaeus, in Long and Sedley (1987: 337).
3 The letter referred to is Spinoza's letter to Jarig Jellis, 2 June 1674 (Letter 50).
4 See Macherey (1979: 142–52) for an interesting account of this aspect of Hegel's comparison between Spinoza's views on individuality and his own.
5 My understanding of this aspect of Hegel's treatment of freedom has benefited from a paper by Robert Pippin (1997) ('Hegel, Freedom, the Will'). Pippin suggests that Hegel's overall project can be described, in contemporary terms, as providing a theory of the possibility of determinate conceptual and judgemental content – a way of understanding the possibiity of judging a thing to be *this* and *that*.
6 Here, as elsewhere throughout her work, Arendt makes a sharp distinction between the political and the ethical. For a helpful discussion of the rationale of the sharpness of Arendt's distinction and of the problems it poses, see Seyla Benhabib (1992).
7 See Balibar (1985: Chapter 1) for an interesting discussion of the bearing on Spinoza's philosophy of the diversity of his own cultural milieu.

4 Theology, politics and norms

1 Letter 19, 5 January 1665, in Curley (1985: 360).
2 Letter L, 2 June 1674, in Spinoza (1955: 369).
3 See Letter 21, 28 January 1665, in Curley (1985: 376).
4 Letter 19, 5 January 1665, in Curley (1985: 360); emphasis added.
5 Blijenbergh's letter to Spinoza, Letter 22, 19 February 1665, in Curley (1985: 385).
6 Letter 23, 13 March 1665, in Curley (1985: 390).

5 Freedom, authority and difference

1 For an analysis of the argument for women's political exclusion in this section of the TP, see Gatens (1996: Chapter 9). See also Matheron (1977).
2 Cornelius Castoriadis has remarked upon the importance of this second nature in the following terms: 'Hegel has said that man is a sick animal. In truth man is a mad animal, totally unfit for life, a species which would have disappeared as soon as it emerged, if it had not proven itself capable, at the collective level, of another creation: society in the strict sense, that is, institutions embodying social imaginary significations' (Castoriadis 1994: 148).
3 In the 'literalist' camp Rice cites Matheron (1969), Zac (1963) and Sacksteder (1980, 1984). In the 'metaphorical' camp he cites Den Uyl (1983) and McShea (1969). Here we are more interested in the opposition between 'literal' and 'metaphorical' than in the details of any particular philosopher's interpretation.
4 As Balibar (1997: 9, n.8) explains, '[b]y individuation I mean that individuals become separated from the environment – which indeed is made of other individuals; by individualization I mean that every individual is unique, or that no such thing as "indiscernible" individuals can exist.'

5 See also Deleuze (1990: 222–3) who makes a similar point with regard to both Spinoza and Leibniz.
6 Heidi Ravven draws attention to this aspect of Spinoza's account of the imagination. She argues that 'imaginative thinking is not only reflective of personal history but precisely both formative of the group and also tradition-bearing. ... Together the two historical aspects of the imagination – one predicated on personal memory and the other on the symbolic rendering of collective memory – make one's mind a reflection of its immediate world and also of that world's common memories' (Ravven, forthcoming).
7 In the TTP Spinoza writes about the effectivity of various 'cultural markers' of identity in creating and maintaining difference across great periods of time. He refers to the Jewish practice of circumcision and to the 'distinctive mark on the heads' of Chinese people (TTP: 56).
8 Under the liberal banner, Taylor, like most other commentators, includes John Rawls, Ronald Dworkin, Thomas Nagel and T.M. Scanlon. See Taylor (1995: Chapter 10).
9 In the communitarian camp, Taylor includes Michael Sandel, Alasdair MacIntyre and Michael Walzer. See Taylor (1995: Chapter 10).

6 Responsibility and the past

1 Letter 91, 4 August 1949, in Kohler and Saner (1992). Quoted in Baier (1993).
2 Epictetus uses the phrase 'citizen of the world' in 'Discourses'. See fragment from Epictetus, 'Discourses', in Long and Sedley (1987: 364).
3 Seneca, *On Leisure*, 4.1, in Long and Sedley (1987: 431). See also Seneca, *On Duties*, I.51: 'The widest association among humans, uniting all among all, is that in which it is necessary to hold in common whatever nature has created for the common use of humans' (quoted in Asmis 1996: 70).
4 For an account of the 'historians' controversy' in Germany, see Maier (1997).
5 We certainly do not mean to imply that dominant groups dominate through the power of the imaginary alone, but rather, that legal, economic and political powers all include an imaginary element. Nor do we propose that recognition of difference can be dealt with independently of the redistribution of social goods. Rather, we claim that participation in the construction of the social imaginary *is* an important social good. Concerning the false antithesis between the politics of recognition and the politics of redistribution, see Fraser (1997: 11–39).
6 There is considerable debate concerning this claim. A former justice of the High Court, Sir Harry Gibbs, has argued that it is misleading to state that the High Court's judgment in *Mabo* rejected *terra nullius*. Gibbs writes: 'The question whether land was *terra nullius* is relevant at international law in deciding whether a state has acquired sovereignty by attempted occupation. So far as I am aware, it was not the question asked at common law to determine whether a colony, admittedly under the sovereignty of Great Britain, was acquired by settlement. Indeed the expression "*terra nullius*" seems to have been unknown to the common law' (Gibbs 1993: xiv). In spite of this learned opinion, historians, indigenous activists and some

lawyers, continue to see *Mabo* as questioning the *legitimacy* of Australian sovereignty.

7 For legal reflections on *Mabo*, see R.H. Bartlett (1993) and Frank Brennan (1995); for an historian's reflections see Henry Reynolds (1996); for an anthropological and interdisciplinary approach, see 'Mabo and Australia', *The Australian Journal of Anthropology*, 6, 1–2.

8 *Ministerial Document Service*, No. 116/92–93, Friday, 11 December 1992, pp. 4790–4.

9 In *Between Past and Future*, Hannah Arendt identifies these disruptions of historical time as demanding a re-thinking of our present. She writes of 'the odd in-between period which sometimes inserts itself into historical time when not only the later historians but actors and witnesses, the living themselves, become aware of an interval in time which is altogether determined by things that are no longer and by things that are not yet. In history, these intervals have shown more than once that they may contain the moment of truth' (Arendt 1961: 9).

10 I am grateful to Paul Patton for bringing this speech to my attention.

Bibliography

Althusser, L. (1997) 'The Only Materialist Tradition, Part I: Spinoza', in W. Montag and T. Stolze (eds) *The New Spinoza*, Minneapolis: University of Minnesota Press.

Anderson, B. (1991) *Imagined Communities*, London: Verso.

Annas, Julia (1993) *The Morality of Happiness*, Oxford: Oxford University Press.

Arendt, H. (1958) *The Human Condition*, Chicago: University of Chicago Press.

Arendt, H. (1961) *Between Past and Future*, London: Faber & Faber.

Arendt, H. (1987) 'Collective Responsibility', in J.W. Bernauer (ed.) *Amor Mundi: Explorations in the Faith and Thought of Hannah Arendt*, Dordrecht: Martinus Nijhoff.

Asmis, E. (1996) 'The Stoics on Women', in J.K. Ward (ed.) *Feminism and Ancient Philosophy*, London: Routledge.

Baier, A. (1993) 'David Hume: Spinozist', *Hume Studies* 19, 2: 237–52.

Balibar, E. (1985) *Spinoza et la politique*, Paris: PUF.

Balibar, E. (1994) 'Spinoza, the Anti-Orwell', in *Masses, Classes, Ideas: Studies on Politics and Philosophy Before and After Marx*, London: Routledge.

Balibar, E. (1997) 'Spinoza: From Individuality to Transindividuality', *Mededelingen vanwege het Spinozahuis*, Delft: Eburon.

Balibar, E. (1998) *Spinoza and Politics*, London and New York: Verso.

Bartlett, R.H. (1993) *The Mabo Decision*, Sydney: Butterworths.

Benhabib, S. (1992) 'Judgment and the Moral Foundations of Politics in Hannah Arendt's Thought', in *Situating the Self: Gender, Community and Postmodernism in Contemporary Ethics*, New York: Routledge.

Benhabib, S. (ed.) (1996) *Democracy and Difference: Contesting the Boundaries of the Political*, Princeton, NJ: Princeton University Press.

Bertrand, Michèle (1983) *Spinoza et l'imaginaire*, Paris: PUF.

Brann, Eva T.H. (1991) *The World of Imagination: Sun and Substance*, Savage, MI: Rowman & Littlefield.

Brennan, F. (1995) *One Land, One Nation: Mabo towards 2001*, St Lucia, Qld: University of Queensland Press.

Cape York Land Council (1997) *The Wik Summit Papers*, Cairns, Qld.

Castoriadis, Cornelius (1994) 'Radical Imagination and the Social Instituting Imaginary', in G. Robinson and J. Rundell (eds) *Rethinking Imagination*, London and New York: Routledge.

Curley, Edwin (ed. and trans.) (1985) *The Collected Works of Spinoza*, Princeton, NJ: Princeton University Press.

Curley, Edwin (ed. and trans.) (1994) *A Spinoza Reader: The Ethics and Other Works*, Princeton, NJ: Princeton University Press.

Curley, E. (1996) 'Kissinger, Spinoza, and Genghis Khan', in D. Garrett (ed.) *The Cambridge Companion to Spinoza*, Cambridge: Cambridge University Press.

Deleuze, Gilles (1988a) *Spinoza: Practical Philosophy*, San Francisco: City Lights Books.

Deleuze, Gilles (1988b) *Foucault*, Minneapolis: University of Minnesota Press.

Deleuze, Gilles (1990) *Expressionism in Philosophy: Spinoza*, New York: Zone Books.

Deleuze, G. and Guattari, F. (1994) *What is Philosophy?*, New York: Columbia University Press.

Den Uyl, D.J. (1983) *Power, State and Freedom: An Interpretation of Spinoza's Political Philosophy*, Assen: Van Gorcum.

Descartes, R. (1985) *The Philosophical Writings of Descartes*, vol. 1, trans. J. Cottingham, R. Stoothoff and D. Murdoch, Cambridge: Cambridge University Press.

Dihle, A. (1982) *The Theory of Will in Classical Antiquity*, Berkeley: University of California Press.

Feuer, L. (1964) *Spinoza and the Rise of Liberalism*, Boston, MA: Beacon Press.

Fraser, N. (1997) *Justice Interruptus: Critical Reflections on the 'Postsocialist' Condition*, New York: Routledge.

Frazer, E. and Lacey, N. (1993) *The Politics of Community: A Feminist Critique of the Liberal-Communitarian Debate*, New York: Harvester Wheatsheaf.

Galichet, F. (1972) 'Le problème de l'illusion chez Spinoza', *Revue Métaphysique et Morale* 77: 1–19.

Gatens, Moira (1996) *Imaginary Bodies: Ethics, Power and Corporeality*, London: Routledge.

Gibbs, H. (1993) 'Foreword', in M. Stephenson and S. Ratnapala (eds) *Mabo: A Judicial Revolution*, St Lucia, Qld: University of Queensland Press.

Hardt, Michael (1995) 'Spinoza's Democracy: The Passions of Social Assemblages', in A. Callari, S. Cullenberg and C. Biewener (eds) *Marxism in the Postmodern Age: Confronting the New World Order*, New York: Guilford Press.

Hegel, G.W.F. (1974) *Lectures on the History of Philosophy*, vol. 3, New York: Humanities Press.

Hegel, G.W.F. (1979) *Hegel's Philosophy of Right*, trans. T.M. Knox, Oxford: Oxford University Press.

Irigaray, L. (1985) *Speculum of the Other Woman*, trans. Gillian C. Gill, Ithaca, NY: Cornell University Press.

James, S. (1996) 'Power and Difference: Spinoza's Conception of Freedom', *The Journal of Political Philosophy* 4, 3: 207–28.

Kohler, L. and Saner, H. (eds) (1992) *Hannah Arendt/Karl Jaspers Correspondence*, New York: Harcourt Brace Jovanovich.

Kymlicka, W. (1990) *Contemporary Political Philosophy*, Oxford: Clarendon Press.

Le Doeuff, M. (1989) *The Philosophical Imaginary*, trans. Colin Gordon, Stanford, CA: Stanford University Press.

Lefort, Claude (1988) 'The Permanence of the Theologico-Political', in *Democracy and Political Theory*, Oxford: Polity Press.

Lloyd, G. (1998) 'Spinoza and the Education of the Imagination', pp. 157–72 in Amélie Rorty (ed.) *Philosophers on Education*, London: Routledge.

Long, A.A. and Sedley, D.N. (eds) (1987) *The Hellensitic Philosophers*, Cambridge: Cambridge University Press.

Lucretius (1975) *De Rerum Natura*, trans. W.H.D. Rouse, Cambridge, MA: Harvard University Press.

Macherey, P. (1979) *Hegel ou Spinoza*, Paris: François Maspero.

Macherey, P. (1992) 'Towards a Natural History of Norms', in *Michel Foucault, Philosopher*, trans. T.J. Armstrong, New York: Harvester Wheatsheaf.

Maier, Charles S. (1997) *The Unmasterable Past*, Cambridge, MA: Harvard University Press.

Matheron, A. (1969) *Individu et communauté chez Spinoza*, Paris: Minuit.

Matheron, A. (1977) 'Spinoza et la sexualité', *Giornale Critico della Filosofia Italiana* 8, 4: 436–57.

McShea, R. (1969) 'Spinoza on Power', *Inquiry* 1, 12: 133–43.

Moens, G.A. (1993) 'Mabo and Political Policy-Making by the High Court', in M. Stephenson and S. Ratnapala (eds) *Mabo: A Judicial Revolution*, St Lucia, Qld: University of Queensland Press.

Negri, A. (1991) *The Savage Anomaly: The Power of Spinoza's Metaphysics and Politics*, trans. M. Hardt, Minneapolis: University of Minnesota Press.

Nietzsche, F. (1973) *Beyond Good and Evil*, trans. R.J. Hollingdale, Harmondsworth: Penguin.

Nussbaum, M. (1996) 'Therapeutic Arguments and Structures of Desire', in J.K. Ward (ed.) *Feminism and Ancient Philosophy*, London: Routledge.

Pettit, Philip (1994) 'Liberal/Communitarian: MacIntyre's Mesmeric Dichotomy', in A. Horton and S. Mendus (eds) *After MacIntyre*, Oxford: Polity Press.

Phillips, A. (1996) 'Dealing with Difference: A Politics of Ideas, or a Politics of Presence?', in S. Benhabib (ed.) *Democracy and Difference*, Princeton, NJ: Princeton University Press.

Pippin, R. (1997) 'Hegel, Freedom, the Will: The Philosophy of Right, 1–33', in Ludwig Siep (ed) *Hegel: Grundlinien der Philosophic des Rechts*, Berlin: Akademic Verlag.

Postema, G. (1991) 'On the Moral Presence of Our Past', *McGill Law Journal* 36, 4: 1155–80.

Puri, K. (1993) 'Copyright Protection for Australian Aborigines in the Light of Mabo', in M. Stephenson and S. Ratnapala (eds) *Mabo: A Judicial Revolution*, St Lucia, Qld: University of Queensland Press.

Ravven, H.M. (forthcoming) 'Spinoza's Rupture with Tradition: On the Character of the Imaginative Life', in H.M. Ravven and L.E. Goodman (eds) *Spinoza and Judaism*, Albany: SUNY.

Reynolds, H. (1996) *Aboriginal Sovereignty: Reflections on Race, State and Nation*, Sydney: Allen & Unwin.

Rice, L.C. (1990) 'Individual and Community: Spinoza's Social Psychology', in E. Curley and P.-F. Moreau (eds) *Spinoza: Issues and Directions*, New York and Leiden: E.J. Brill.

Ricoeur, Paul (1994) 'Imagination in Discourse and in Action', in J. Rundell and G. Robinson (eds) *Rethinking Imagination*, London: Routledge. (Originally published in *Analecta Husserliana*, vol. VII, 1978, 3–22.)

Rorty, R. (1984) 'The Historiography of Philosophy: Four Genres', in R. Rorty, J.B. Schneewind and Q. Skinner (eds) *Philosophy in History*, Cambridge: Cambridge University Press.

Sacksteder, W. (1975) 'Spinoza on Democracy', in E. Freeman and M. Mandelbaum (eds) *Spinoza: Essays in Interpretation*, La Salle: Open Court.

Sacksteder, W. (1980) 'Spinoza on Part and Whole: The Worm's Eye View', *Southwest Journal of Philosophy* 11: 25–40.

Sacksteder, W. (1984) 'Communal Orders in Spinoza', in C. De Deugd (ed.) *Spinoza's Political and Theological Thought*, Amsterdam: North-Holland.

Scott, J. (1995) 'Multiculturalism and the Politics of Identity', in J. Rajchman (ed.) *The Identity in Question*, New York and London: Routledge.

Scruton, Roger (1986) *Spinoza*, Oxford: Oxford University Press.

Seneca (1989) *Ad Lucilium Epistulae Morales I*, trans. R.M. Gummere (Loeb Classical Library), Cambridge, MA: Harvard University Press.

Sepper, D. (1996) *Descartes's Imagination: Proportion, Images and the Activity of Thinking*, Berkeley: University of California Press.

Smith, Steven B. (1997) *Spinoza, Liberalism, and the Question of Jewish Identity*, New Haven, CT: Yale University Press.

Spinoza, B. (1951) *A Theologico-Political Treatise and A Political Treatise*, trans. R.H.M. Elwes, New York: Dover.

Spinoza, B. (1955) *On the Improvement of Human Understanding: The Ethics and Selected Letters*, trans. R.H.M. Elwes, New York: Dover.

Strauss, Leo (1997) *Spinoza's Critique of Religion* [1965], Chicago and London: University of Chicago Press.

Taylor, Charles (1995) *Philosophical Arguments*, Cambridge, MA: Harvard University Press.

Tully, J. (1995) *Strange Multiplicity: Constitutionalism in an Age of Diversity*, Cambridge: Cambridge University Press.

Williams, B. (1993) *Shame and Necessity*, Berkeley: University of California Press.

Yovel, Yirmiyahu (1989a) *Spinoza and Other Heretics*, vol. 1: *The Marrano of Reason*, Princeton, NJ: Princeton University Press.

Yovel, Yirmiyahu (1989b) *Spinoza and Other Heretics*, vol. 2: *The Adventures of Immanence*, Princeton, NJ: Princeton University Press.

Zac, S. (1963) *L'Idée de vie dans la philosophie de Spinoza*, Paris: PUF.

Index